D0921207

Living Trusts for Everyone:
A Common Sense Approach
to
Protecting You, Your Assets
and Your Family

by

Michael J. Hainer and Dennis M. Brown

ISBN 0-9713455-0-3   24.95

The information in this book is for informational and educational purposes only. Nothing in this book shall be considered to be rendering legal or other advice for specified estate planning cases or otherwise. Further, the authors are not engaged in rendering legal, tax, accounting or similar professional services. While legal, tax and accounting issues covered in this book have been checked with sources believed to be reliable, some material may be affected by changes in the law or in the interpretations of such laws since the manuscript for this book was completed. For that reason, the accuracy and completeness of such information, and any opinions based thereon, is not guaranteed. In addition, state or local tax laws or procedural rules may have a material impact on the general statements made by the authors, and the general strategies outlined in this book may not be suitable for every individual.

All readers are responsible for obtaining their own legal, accounting, investment and other expert advice from experienced practitioners in those fields in connection with preparing their own estate plan.

The authors and publishers shall have neither liability nor responsibility to any person or entity with respect to any loss or damage caused or alleged to be caused directly or indirectly by the information contained in this book.

If you do not wish to be bound by the above, you may return the book to the publisher for a full refund.

Except as permitted under the United States Copyright Act of 1976, no part of this publication may be reproduced or distributed in any form or by any means or stored in a data base or retrieval system, without the prior written permission of the authors.

Inquiries regarding this book should be addressed to:

National Association of Advisors to Seniors, LLC
2841 Monroe, Suite 11
Dearborn, MI 48124
(800) 428-4825

Published in the United States of America

ACKNOWLEDGEMENTS

There are literally dozens of people we want to thank for this book. Our respective office staffs deserve special mention for having put up with us for so long. To those at Hainer & Berman, P.C., particularly Karen Mullins, Mike Hainer's sister, many, many thanks for your never ending support over the years. To those on Dennis Brown's staff at M & O, many thanks for putting up with the excitable Dennis all these years and to our respective partners, Len Berman and Tim Otto, who had the misfortune (or good fortune) to work with us over the years.

DEDICATION

Because we have so many people to thank, we each have included our own dedication.

Michael J. Hainer

First and foremost, I would like to dedicate this book to my wife, Susan, and my three daughters, January, Tracy and Shelley, for the numerous sacrifices they have made over the years. Many family events have been cancelled or postponed so I could attend to the needs of my clients—clients who in many cases have become members of our extended family. Thank you for your love, patience, understanding and support.

I would also like to thank my mother, Arline Robbins, and my grandmother, Bertha Tracy. My mother taught my sisters and me the value of hard work and perseverance. We did not have a lot of money, but we always had a lot of love. Like many New Englanders, Gram Bert worked hard her whole life, scrimping and saving to make ends meet. She initially worked as a potato picker in northern Maine and later as a maid in Bangor, Maine, while raising six children on her own; I never heard her complain once. The lessons I learned from my mom and grandmother are far more valuable than the ones I learned at Michigan Law School.

Also, special thanks to my wife's parents, Joe and June Romaine, who extended a helping hand many times over the past 25 years. I would also like to dedicate this book to my two sisters, Kathy, who left us much too soon, and Karen who worked 12 hours a day to help my law firm get off the ground over eleven years ago.

Finally, I would like to dedicate this book to my co-author, Dennis Brown. Dennis and I grew up together in Southgate, Michigan, a middle-class, blue-collar neighborhood outside of Detroit. We weren't poor, but we certainly were not rich. While we never really had many material possessions, we didn't really care because we had the things we needed: we could play baseball in the summer, football in the fall, and street hockey in the spring. We have been friends since we were 12 years old—a friendship I cherish more with each passing day.

For years, Dennis has been after me to co-author a book with him that would provide practical advice to people just like our parents—average everyday folks who get up every morning and go to work. These are people who, through hard work, accumulate a nice little nest egg they want to pass on to their children. This is that book. Dennis, thanks for keeping after me so we could make your dream a reality.

Dennis M. Brown

To my Lord and God, Savior and Friend, Jesus Christ
Through you all things are possible. You have blessed me abundantly throughout my 47 years. Nothing would be the same without you as the core of my life. Trusting in you has helped me to accept the paths I have taken, and to be grateful and happy with every small, large and difficult step. I love you above all things, and I thank you for touching my life with all the good people and wonderful gifts you have created.

To my life partner, confidant, counselor and bride Denise
I dedicate all the positive results this book will have on those who read it. You have stood by me, supported and believed in me when our times were at their toughest. Together we have shared many personal triumphs. From you I have learned to share the gifts that God has blessed me with, to be persistent when faced with obstacles and, most importantly, to always be proud of what I do and of who I am. Your love sustains me. Each day, I thank the Lord for you. I will forever love you.

To Ryan, Daniel, Sarah, Julia and Olivia my beautiful children
Of all the gifts given to me by God, you are my most treasured. I am grateful to God for giving me the privilege of being called your Dad. Through you I have come to understand the true meaning of unconditional love. I am proud of all of you, and of the fine human beings you are becoming.

To Dan Rourke
A very special thank you. My personal and professional life is touched each day by your wisdom, generosity and your sharing of yourself.

To my partner; Tim Otto
Thank you for sharing your insight, patience and honesty with me.

To my friend and co-author, Mike Hainer, with whom I continue to share the sparkle and vigor of our youth. I am extremely indebted to you and grateful for your unselfish labor in helping me through the details and the nuisance and contents of this book.

To all the people who have touched my life in one-way or another; I thank you.

TABLE OF CONTENTS

I.

<u>INTRODUCTION: A ROAD MAP</u>

The AARP estimates that $2,000,000,000 (that's two billion dollars) are spent annually on probate costs and expenses, including executor fees, attorneys fees, appraisers, inventory fees, filing fees and related expenses. This book will show you how to greatly reduce or completely avoid these and other expenses by establishing a Living Trust. However, as you will quickly learn, avoiding probate is but one benefit of a Living Trust.

This book begins by providing you with a brief chapter on the reasons you should read this book (as compared with watching re-runs or another football game). We trust you will agree with us and keep reading. Chapter III tells you what other experts are saying about Living Trusts.

Chapter IV is a key chapter; it provides over ten real world examples of how a Living Trust solves real world problems. Many of these examples involve situations where a person failed to establish a Living Trust. Hopefully, you will learn from their attendance at the school of hard knocks and not repeat their mistakes because of indifference or avoidance. If you read nothing else, you should read Chapter IV.

Chapter V takes a more detailed look at the Living Trust and the rest of the key estate planning documents by describing the technical aspects of a Living Trust. Chapter VI explains how the Living Trust relates to ordinary folks—not only the rich and famous. Chapter VII provides a detailed look at the major benefits of a Living Trust. Chapter VIII describes the remaining documents in your estate planning package and describes the interrelationship between those documents and the Living Trust.

Up until this point, the benefits of a Living Trust (and a good estate planning package) apply to all persons. However, if your estate—the assets you own, including life insurance and retirement benefits—is greater than $675,000, Living Trusts can be used to save estate taxes. Chapter IX will show you how Living Trusts can save taxes on the first $1,375,000 (increasing to $2,000,000) that you give to your loved ones.

We then back up a bit and talk more extensively about probate in Chapter X, and then, in Chapter XI, how to transfer assets to the Living Trust.

One amazing statistic is that 70% of all Americans will die without doing any estate planning. Though there may be many reasons for this phenomenon, we believe a significant contributing factor is that the typical person does not know how to find a good estate planning lawyer. Chapter XII provides you with our thoughts on that subject. We conclude by covering frequently asked questions regarding Living Trusts (Chapter XIII). We have also included a glossary of key terms and an appendix of sample estate planning documents so you can see how the actual documents look.

Finally, let us tell you what this book does not cover. This book is directed at the benefits of the revocable Living Trust for people whose assets range from $100,000 to approximately $2,000,000 to $2,500,000. Those people with assets in excess of that amount have some special planning opportunities that are beyond the scope of the book. Such estate planning opportunities include irrevocable life insurance trusts, generation skipping trusts, family limited partnerships, limited liability companies, charitable remainder trusts, and a number of other estate planning techniques. These topics are beyond the scope of this book. If you would like some additional information on these topics, please feel free to contact us at the address shown at the beginning of the book. We will be happy to help you.

We have worked very hard to create a book that is both easy to read and easy to use as a reference source. In short, we have tried to discuss the practical benefits of a Living Trust and minimize the legalese. However, while reading it from cover to cover, you may notice some points were repeated. We have repeated them for several reasons:

1. The concepts, for the most part, are new to many of the readers and therefore need to be explained more than once.

2. Those points are the most important ones and deserve repetition. (In fact, most people need to see or hear a fact more than three times to learn it and then remember it.)

3. By providing the same, or substantially similar, information in more than one place, the explanations will, hopefully, be understandable for you.

We suggest you read the entire book all the way through, just as you would read a story. If you find a paragraph to be repetitious, just skip over it and go on to the next paragraph. You will appreciate the completeness when you refer to specific points.

These pages can truly change your life. Most importantly, you will save your family the pain and agony that will almost certainly result if you do not put your affairs in order. Please do two things to help them:

1) Read this book.

2) Implement your estate plan.

©DG 1990

II.

WHY YOU SHOULD READ THIS BOOK

You should read this book for several very important reasons. First, you should read this book if you are interested in saving money. The American Association of Retired People ("AARP") has estimated that 70% of all Americans will die without having an estate plan in place. AARP estimates that two billion dollars will be lost annually to the costs and expenses associated with the probate process. These costs and expenses take the form of personal representative or executor fees, attorney fees, probate/inventory fees and appraisal costs. AARP estimates that conservatively **three to eight percent** of your assets will be wasted through the probate process.

We have written this book to stop this carnage—this tremendous waste of money. In earlier times, everybody had a will, which would transfer assets upon their death to their loved ones. **In most cases, in this new millennium, a will is not the most cost-effective way to transfer assets.** A will is simply an outdated tool for the transfer of assets to your loved ones, which is, for most of you, the principal concern. The simple truth is that, with the advent of computerization and increased specialization in the legal and financial services industries, your assets can be transferred to your loved ones more cost effectively by using a revocable trust in almost every case.

A Living Trust has numerous other benefits: avoiding probate court in the event of incapacity, controlling and delaying distributions after your death to your children and/or grandchildren, preserving your privacy, and minimizing federal and state estate taxes. All of these benefits and others will be discussed in more detail later in the book.

Secondly, you should read this book because, unlike your parents, you have a substantial amount of money to transfer to your children, grandchildren or other loved ones. Many of you have saved your entire life and now have hundreds of thousands, if not millions, of dollars to transfer to your children and grandchildren. As your situation is not the same as your parents, the tools needed to transfer those assets are also not the same. Just think about it: 401(k) accounts and IRAs did not exist for your parents. In most cases, they lived in one house their entire lives; today, people have lived in many homes and, in many instances, have a vacation home, often in a different state. Today, after ten years of a bull market, many people have more money to leave their heirs than they ever dreamed. This new wealth needs to be treated with much more care than the care taken with the few assets your parents left to you.

Many of you may still think that a revocable trust is too "fancy" for you. However, advancements in technology have made the will virtually obsolete for transferring ownership of property. **A revocable Living Trust, due to technology, is the most cost effective means of transferring ownership of property by people— truly, the estate planning tool for the next millennium. And, as you will see, a Living Trust solves a number of estate planning problems for you even if your estate is not substantial.**

Some of you may be resistant to change. However, change is often positive. Few people would argue that the world is worse off today because we invented the automobile or the computer. Does anyone really want to go back to the horse and buggy or to the abacus?

A simple will is essentially today's horse and buggy. This is not to say that probate courts do not have their place. In fact, probate courts have greatly simplified their procedures in recent years to try to reduce the cost of having to probate assets. Moreover, there will always be a need for probate courts to resolve disputes regarding a person's estate. For example, a child born out of wedlock may believe that he was unintentionally disinherited. However, generally, you do not have to waste money going to probate court to transfer your assets.

Third, you should read this book because you owe it to your family to have your affairs in order. You may not want to think about it, but you are certainly going to die. And you might become disabled. And you may end up in a nursing home. And your spouse may remarry. And your children may not always get along perfectly. You owe it to your spouse and your family to make sure your affairs are in order. You can avoid the heartache, the invasion of privacy, and the arguments that often take place when someone dies without putting their affairs in order. Some people say, "what do I care, I will be dead." If you are one of those people—and really believe it—put the book down and go watch TV; we can't help you. But I would guess most of you don't subscribe to that philosophy. You were not raised that way and neither were your children. Your ingrained values give you the backbone to do the right thing—not because it is necessarily fun (although a good lawyer with a sense of humor can make it tolerable).

As Gram Bert used to say, "you burned your butt, and now you have to sit on the blisters." Trust us, if you don't put your affairs in order, your family will be sitting on the blisters.

III.

WHAT THE OTHER EXPERTS ARE SAYING

As you will see, the Living Trust (when part of an overall estate and financial plan) serves many functions and eliminates many problems when you are alive and when you pass away. Because of its flexibility, the Living Trust is truly the estate planning tool for the next thousand years. We are not alone in our views. Here are a few opinions of other experts in this field.

"The advantages of Living Trusts over wills are considerable. Under a will, an estate must be settled in probate court. Lawyers' fees and court costs often are substantial: there may be exasperating delays, and the proceedings are a matter of public record. In contrast, a Living Trust is settled without a court proceeding: a Successor Trustee simply distributes assets according to the trust's instructions, with an accountant, notary public or lawyer certifying any transfer of titles. The process is much quicker, cheaper and more private than settling a will, and it may save on estate taxes."

— The Wall Street Journal

"...the revocable Living Trust has even more features that make it the most versatile and effective estate planning technique available."

— Robert A. Esperti, atty. and Renno L. Peterson, atty., authors of *The Living Trust Revolution*

"The Living Trust makes the old-fashioned will obsolete ... eliminates estate-devouring probate charges and attorney's fees, speeds up the distribution of funds to your heirs by months or even years . . . is totally revocable — allowing you to change your mind at anytime, legally valid in all 50 states."

— Henry W. Abts, author of *The Living Trust*

"The probate process may be completed in only six months, or go on for several years, if complications arise. The average time needed to complete probate varies from state to state, and from estate to estate, but is generally one year."

— AARP report, "Wills & Living Trusts"

"...the real advantage [of a Living Trust] is not upon death, but during life ... It is an excellent vehicle for older people who fear illness or incapacity."

— The Wall Street Journal

"There are four major reasons why people — many of them ordinary folks and not just the fabulously wealthy — establish trusts . . . The first is to preserve and protect your estate from the predations of the Internal Revenue Service . . . The second reason is to avoid probate, the often messy and very public affair by which a court tests and evaluates how your assets are passed on to your beneficiaries after your death. The third reason for a trust is that you want a prudent, expert third party . . . to manage [your] assets . . . The fourth is anticipation of incapacity, such as Alzheimer's."

— Marshall Loeb, "Not Just for Leisure Class. Trusts Can Be Useful for Middle-Income Americans, Too." cbs.marketwatch.com July 26, 2000

"The best way to avoid probate court costs and delays is to have a Living Trust for major assets. The advantages far outweigh the slight disadvantages."

— Robert J. Bruss, The Repository; Canton, Ohio

"The activities that occur routinely in some probate courts have created a negative image — long delays, inordinate costs associated with settling an estate, lack of privacy, and sometimes, lawsuits over provisions in a will."

— Merle Dowd, columnist with The Seattle Times

IV.

THE SCHOOL OF HARD KNOCKS:
HOW A LIVING TRUST SOLVES PROBLEMS
IN THE REAL WORLD

Most of you could care less about the legal nuances and intricacies of a Living Trust. You want to know how a Living Trust can solve your particular problems. Accordingly, we begin this book with examples of how a Living Trust did or could have saved a person's hard earned money or spared his family anguish.

My father-in-law calls these experiences learning from the "school of hard knocks." Hopefully, you will learn from the little history lesson we are providing and not doom yourself to repeat their mistakes. Obviously, names (and, in certain circumstances, details) have been changed to preserve confidences. Later on, we explore a few of the technical aspects of a Living Trust.

THE STUBBORN FATHER

Bob just wouldn't listen to his daughter, Mary. His wife had been dead for several years now, but he refused to go see a lawyer about updating his Simple Will and having a Living Trust prepared. Unfortunately, Bob had assets, including real estate, in two different states because he spent the winters in Florida. When he died, two probate administrations had to be opened: one in Michigan and one in Florida. Even though his assets were relatively modest, less then $250,000 in total, his estate had to pay two lawyers—one in each state—to handle the probate administration. In addition, his estate had to pay inventory fees to both probate courts. Even using the simplified probate procedures, the cost greatly exceeded the cost of setting up a Living Trust, and delayed the distribution of assets for several months longer than would have been the case with a Living Trust. In addition, Mary, who was the Personal Representative, had twice the work. Bob could have avoided this hardship on Mary, while saving money, by setting up a Living Trust.

DID YOU KNOW THIS FACT: Most assets you own in your name at your death (except those with beneficiary designations) have to go through probate court to transfer those assets to your beneficiaries. In addition, if you own real estate in another state (such as a vacation home), a second probate administration—called an ancillary probate—will need to take place in that state. Hence, twice the fees. In many cases, these fees are unrelated to the amount of money at stake; for example, it may take the lawyer the same amount of time to transfer a mobile home and lot worth $20,000 as it would to transfer a million dollar condo for one of his wealthy clients. Since most lawyers charge on a per hour basis, generally ranging from $150 to $350 per hour, the costs are disproportionate to the value of the assets transferred.

OPINION: In our opinion, most single people should have a Living Will to avoid going through probate. This is doubly true when property is owned in more than one state. By using a Living Trust, you maintain control while you are alive and avoid probate in both states when you die. Upon your death, the Successor Trustee, who you also will choose, distributes the assets without delay in accordance with your instructions.

THE DOUBLE WHAMMY

Laurie had $800,000 of assets that her husband, Harold, had left her several years earlier. (The assets had almost doubled in value since he died). Because Harold had always taken care of Laurie, she never got around to seeing an estate planning lawyer.

She knew her simple will left all the money to their children equally. She kept asking her friends what was the "big deal about this Living Trust." Unfortunately, before she took the time to discover the answer, she was stricken with Alzheimer's disease and was soon living in a nursing home, paying $4,500 a month for her care. Before she was admitted, however, the nursing home required someone to sign as the "responsible party" for her. No one was crazy enough to do that, particularly since none of her kids were rich and most of them lived out of the state. In addition, the kids had no idea how much of their mother's money was involved.

To solve this problem, her son living in state, Ken, had to hire a lawyer to apply to the Probate Court to be appointed Guardian and Conservator for Laurie—first on a temporary basis to get her into the nursing home and then, later, on a permanent basis, after the Court held a formal hearing. (In this case, the Court also appointed an independent third party—called a guardian ad litem—to evaluate Laurie to make sure she needed a guardian and conservator.) Laurie bore the cost of these proceedings, which were totally unnecessary and cost several thousand dollars in attorney fees, fees paid to the Guardian Ad Litem, and court costs. In addition, Ken had to publicly disclose all of Laurie's assets and file annual accountings with the court showing how the assets were spent each year—all at great expense and inconvenience. Most of us, like Laurie, would have shuddered at the thought of the whole world looking in at our affairs.

NOTE: These proceedings were not even contested; if the kids had disagreed over whom should control Laurie's affairs or if Laurie had fought the appointment of a guardian because she did not feel she needed one—both of which happen all the time in the real world—the expense would have increased geometrically. For example, there would be competing testimony on which child deserved to be Laurie's guardian and conservator, and testimony from doctors about whether she was competent.

Laurie languished in the nursing home for several years. During that period of time, she made several trips to the hospital for her heart attacks that were becoming increasing more severe; on her last trip, the doctors pulled Ken aside and asked if Laurie has executed a Medical Power of Attorney and Living Will, which authorized the termination of life support if her situation was terminable and death was imminent. Ken, of course, had neither, but being a court-appointed Guardian gave him the power to make that decision—albeit an expensive method of getting that authority. Unfortunately, Ken had no idea what to do with this "power," having never discussed the matter with his mother. His brothers and sisters were at each other's throats over what "Mom would have wanted," and relationships were progressively more strained and "ugly" within the family. Ken, for his part, thought his brother Fred had mixed motives, since he desperately needed money to cover losses from his failed business venture. Then Laurie passed away in the night, sparing the siblings more painful arguments.

At that point, the guardianship and conservatorship terminated as a matter of law. Guess what! Ken had to go back to Probate Court to have himself appointed as Personal Representative for his mother's affairs under the will. In the interim, until he was given letters of authority, he could not even access the accounts of his mother where he, as guardian and conservator, had had access for years. The bills kept coming. Laurie's estate had to pay the attorneys (again) to file the paper work and pay an inventory fee of several thousand dollars on the assets being transferred to the children. In addition, as part of the process, an inventory had to be filed with the probate court, which disclosed all of Laurie's assets. Most, if not all, of these costs and expenses could have been avoided if Laurie had only seen a competent estate planning attorney.

Further, the assets then had to be transferred to the children. Only one problem: one of Laurie's children had predeceased her and the will did not state clearly who was to take the share of the deceased child (i.e. would that share go to his (the deceased's) brothers and sisters or to his children—Laurie's grandchildren). After a nasty court hearing, and several tens of thousands of dollars of attorney fees, the court distributed the money to the grandchildren.

DID YOU KNOW THIS FACT: A Durable Power of Attorney is created while you are competent. It authorizes someone you trust to make decisions regarding your affairs and assets, to pay your bills and to handle your investments when you are unable to do so on your own. It is inexpensive and usually included as part of any complete estate plan from an experienced estate planning lawyer. The Durable Power of Attorney works hand in hand with your Living Trust because usually the person named as your Successor Trustee is the same as the person named as your agent under your Durable Power of Attorney. If Laurie had secured a Living Will and a Durable Power of Attorney, she could have avoided the cost and expense of having a guardian and conservator appointed by the Probate Court. She also would have avoided the public disclosures required.

DID YOU KNOW THIS FACT: Under the laws of many states, you can execute a Healthcare or Medical Power of Attorney which allows someone to make medical decisions for you if you are incapacitated or otherwise unable to make those decisions. In addition, you may also execute a Living Will, which authorizes medical authorities to terminate life-sustaining measures under limited circumstances, such as when you have a terminal condition. Although a Living Will may not be technically enforceable in most states, as a practical matter, doctors will often recognize the document in making decisions because it expresses a person's wishes, particularly when the Living Will was prepared in advance. In other states, life-sustaining measures may only be discontinued if the person expresses this decision in a Living Will. These documents are usually prepared as part of a complete estate planning package.

With a Medical Power of Attorney and a Living Will, Laurie could have avoided a lot of heartache for her family; Ken and all the other children would have known her wishes.

DID YOU KNOW THIS FACT: Guardianship and conservatorship remains in effect only while the incompetent person is alive or until the person regains his or her competence. When the person dies, access to the money and to the assets is immediately halted, and the probate process begins. In most states, as in the state Ken resided, after the will is admitted to probate, the personal representative or executor is appointed and receives what is called "letters of authority." Until Ken received those letters of authority he did not have the right of access to any of mom's accounts to pay debts and distribute assets.

OPINION: The days of seeing your good friend, the corner-store lawyer are long gone. The rules regarding trusts, estates and tax laws are becoming more complex by the day. You should hire an experienced estate planner to minimize the risk of ambiguity in your document. Look what happened to Laurie. Ambiguity leads to lawsuits—expensive lawsuits.

PENNY WISE AND POUND FOOLISH

Sally, a widow, set up an appointment with her lawyer four times. Each time she cancelled the appointment because she did not think it was worth the money. After all, she wasn't rich; she and her husband had just been working class people, who scrimped and saved all their lives. Those trusts were "too fancy." Boy, was she wrong! Her husband had left her approximately $650,000, plus the house, which was worth $110,000. She was doing fine on his pension and social security; she never touched the other money. She had placed most of her assets in joint ownership names with the kids. Unfortunately, all of the kids were not on each of the accounts. One daughter, Pat, held $300,000 jointly with Sally; she held a $200,000 account with daughter Sandy, and a $150,000 account with both Pat and her son, Rob. Sally also had eight grandchildren whom she loved dearly. There was also a simple will that divided everything equally among the kids. The house was still in Sally's and her husband's name, but she had told her daughter Pat, but not the others, that she wanted Sandy to get it. Sally also had some Series E bonds, worth $5,000, and a small checking account that were both in her name alone. In addition, she had a $4,000 life insurance policy; her husband had been named as the sole beneficiary. At the time she died, a federal estate tax return had to be filed because the assets exceeded $600,000 (the exempt amount at the time).

Thus, when Sally died, her estate was a mess. First, the children met with the same lawyer their mother had avoided meeting when she was alive. Of course, a probate estate had to be opened, with the usual costs and expenses of filing the paperwork, having a personal representative appointed, obtaining letters of authority, filing inventory, publishing a claims notice so any creditors could file claims with the probate court, and paying inventory fees as well as other paperwork to open and close the estate. All these actions were a tremendous waste of time and money.

More importantly, the distribution of assets was a mess. Sally's plan—whatever it was—was not well thought out or executed. As a matter of law, jointly held assets actually belong to the survivor, which meant that the assets would have not been divided equally, as her will stated. In addition, under the will, the house probably would have been sold with the proceeds divided equally and not given to her daughter, Sandy.

After a little teeth gnashing and several meetings, the kids totally reorganized what their mother had done—or failed to do—and redistributed the assets among themselves equally. However, the cost of doing so, plus the fees and expenses of probate, greatly exceeded what would have been paid had a Living Trust been set up in the first place. One can only imagine the lawsuits and hard feelings if the children—with influence from their spouses—had simply kept the money they were entitled to, as a matter of law under the joint accounts, or had sold the house and distributed the proceeds.

The larger crime was the wasted opportunity to save taxes, accounting and attorneys' fees. Sally was living just fine on her pension and social security. Accordingly, over the years, she could have gifted away assets ($10,000 per each person) to her children, their spouses and her grandchildren to reduce her estate to a level where no federal or state estate taxes were due and, therefore, there would have been no need to pay accountants and lawyers to prepare the various returns.

DID YOU KNOW THIS FACT: By law, a person whose name is on an account or asset actually has an ownership interest in the account or asset—which is probably not what most people think is the situation when they set up joint accounts with their children. For example, most brokerage accounts can not be closed without the signature of both parties to an account. Moreover, there is technically a gift created which could create liability for gift taxes if the gift is in excess of $10,000. Most importantly, the jointly owned asset passes on to the survivor when you die. Thus, your will does not even affect jointly owned assets, and they often end up going to the wrong person. A better solution is to place the assets into a Living Trust—which you alone control while you are alive—and then the assets will be distributed according to your wishes in the Living Trust when you die.

DID YOU KNOW THIS FACT: Life insurance avoids probate if the primary beneficiary is alive. If the primary beneficiary is not alive and no contingent beneficiary is named, the money is usually payable to the estate. A better solution is to name your Living Trust as the beneficiary. The money is then distributed outside probate. In addition, a well-drafted Living Trust will clearly specify who gets the money (including insurance proceeds) if the other spouse or one of the children dies (and therefore, you do not need to change beneficiaries repeatedly). Finally, life insurance is usually exempt from claims of creditors if made payable to the Living Trust, but it is not exempt from claims of creditors if paid to your estate.

OPINION: Most people underestimate the value of their assets. In addition, there is a real hesitancy to meet with a lawyer. In our area, most lawyers will meet with you free for the first hour; sit down with the lawyer and see if you are compatible. Assuming the first meeting goes fine, you are all set. Here, Sally could have saved her family thousands of dollars in taxes, fees and expenses by visiting a lawyer. (See Chapter XII for more details in selecting a lawyer.)

BEWARE THE JOINT TENANT

An elderly widow, Margaret, had one daughter, Sue, who she wished to inherit everything. Rather than create a Living Trust, Sue was added as a joint tenant on all of Margaret's bank accounts, and to the ownership of Margaret's condominium. At the time Margaret added Sue's name to her assets, Sue was a responsible adult. However, she then fell into alcoholism and drug use and became intimate with a small time drug dealer who thoroughly entrenched her in drug use; Sue lost her job and spent all of her money on drugs.

When Sue's money was gone, the boyfriend convinced her to tap into her mother's accounts to feed her habit, and he ultimately persuaded Sue to sell her half interest in her mother's condominium to buy drugs. When her mother learned about the sale, she was forced to hire lawyers to file an action to "quiet title" to her condominium. The monies taken out of Margaret's accounts by Sue were long gone—never to be recovered since Sue was a joint tenant. Fortunately, her mother was able to persuade the court to reinstate her title in the condominium. However, it was an expensive lesson to say the least.

DID YOU KNOW THIS FACT: As previously discussed, a person whose name is on an account or asset actually has an ownership interest in that account or asset. As Margaret found out, joint tenancy has many negative consequences. While not everyone's child turns into a drug addict, they certainly may get divorced, end up in a car accident, or file for bankruptcy. Those things happen every day in America, particularly with 50% of all marriages ending in divorce. Again, the better solution is to place the assets into a Living Trust—which you alone control while you are alive—and then the assets will be distributed according to your wishes, specified in the Living Trust, when you die.

DID YOU KNOW THIS FACT: Most older married couples travel together. In addition, many older couples hold their assets as joint tenants, believing they can avoid the necessity of a will and Living Trust. This approach is usually not sound for several reasons. First, joint tenancy only delays probate—with its attendant costs, delays and expenses—until after the first to die. Second, your estate planning matters are usually better handled when both are alive and healthy since usually only one spouse handles the family's financial affairs on a regular basis. The estate planning process allows both spouses to become familiar with these important matters.

In our experience, most spouses do not want the surviving spouse to go through these difficult issues alone. Third, without a will or a Living Trust, you die "intestate"—which means without a will—and your assets are distributed as the state statutes prescribe. Often, the distribution scheme is not consistent with your wishes. If both of you die together in a car accident, your plans for your joint assets go down the drain and the assets will go through probate, the State deciding where your assets will go. Moreover, because most seniors spend a lot of time traveling together, this risk is not insignificant.

THE TWO SISTERS

Two sisters, Jane and Jackie, were divorced; each had children in their late twenties and early thirties. They were very close and, therefore, put all of their accounts in joint names, except for their houses, which remained in their own names. One sister, Jackie, traveled extensively outside of the U.S. They trusted each other, but were still hesitant to give authority to their children who were still maturing. In this case, to avoid any joint tenancy problems while giving each of them the rights to the other's accounts, we set up a Living Trust for each of them where both served as Co-Trustees from the beginning (just like a joint account without the problems) and we put all assets in the Living Trust, including the house. Thus, they had all the benefits of joint accounts without any of the problems previously discussed.

THE STEEL WORKER AND HIS LOVING FAMILY

This is a similar story, but it shows the flexibility of a Living Trust. Bob and his wife, Betty, had lived a long and productive life. They were married for over 50 years, raising three lovely children, all of whom had themselves raised lovely families. Bob and Betty were not rich. However, they were living comfortably on their pensions and there was no mortgage on the house. Because their health was failing, their kids were already helping them by paying the bills (i.e. they were making out the checks for their mom and dad to sign). Bob and Betty wanted to make sure that their money was divided equally among their three kids when they died. However, they wanted to treat some of the grandchildren differently (and make gifts to Bob and Betty's siblings) if Bob and Betty's children died before them. Their current estate plan, a simple will, did not match their current desires. To make matters worse, some of their children's names were on some joint accounts, and some of the other children were named on other joint accounts.

In this case, the Living Trust fit the bill to the tee. All of their assets were transferred into the Living Trust, and their three children were named as current Co-Trustees while Betty and Bob were alive so that they could help with mom and dad's affairs in the present. In addition, each child was given immediate power, along with mom and dad, under the Durable Powers of Attorney and Health Care Powers of Attorneys (a specific power of attorney that relates to health care matters). By implementing this estate plan, the children were able to help their parents immediately and the joint tenancy problems described above were avoided. In addition, we were able to draft the Living Trust to account for the different distributions depending upon who was alive at the time of their death or deaths.

SMOOTH TRANSITION

A loving daughter took her mother to have her estate plan prepared, which included a Pour Over Will, a Living Trust, a Durable Power of Attorney, a Medical Power of Attorney and a Living Will. The Living Trust basically divided her assets between the daughter and her brother. All of the assets, which were less than $300,000, were put into the Trust. The mother went into a nursing home where she lived for several years. The daughter took care of her mother using her powers under the Living Trust and the Durable and Medical Powers of Attorney. Most of her mother's assets were used up to pay the nursing home; all that was left was $20,000. After her mother died, the daughter called her mother's attorney to see what she needed to do. The response: (a) pay the funeral home; (b) file your mom's last tax return and pay any tax (there was not any); and (c) distribute the rest between you and your brother. There was no need for any further legal action (and there was no charge for the call). Not all matters are this simple, but you can see the ease with which these matters can be handled with a Living Trust—all while maintaining privacy and dignity.

THE RETIREMENT ACCOUNTS DILEMMA: YOU CAN'T GET TO IT

Richard and Mary had virtually all of their net worth in retirement accounts (IRA and 401k accounts). In fact, they used that money for living expenses. They thought they didn't need an estate plan since they were going to leave their accounts to each other. Nothing could be further from the truth. If one of them became disabled, the other could not take money out of the disabled person's retirement account. The solution was to prepare a Durable Power of Attorney and a Living Trust, both of which provide that, upon disability, the other person can access the accounts. Your Durable Power of Attorney and Living Trust should make very clear that your retirement accounts can be accessed; otherwise, your loved ones will not be able to access the accounts when they need them the most—to pay medical and household bills when their partner is disabled.

DID YOU KNOW THIS FACT: Some financial institutions will not honor a Durable Power of Attorney unless it is drawn on their own form. Moreover, even if a financial institution will accept your Durable Power of Attorney, the financial institution will almost always require that your signature on your Durable Power of Attorney be "Signature Guaranteed" by a bank or other financial institution. Without a "Signature Guarantee," the Durable Power of Attorney may be worthless.

OPINION: Your should also be certain that your Durable Power of Attorney and Living Trust allows your successor to make gifts to those loved ones that qualify for the annual exemption amount (currently $10,000 per donee per year). This power gives your agent and trustee the ability to make gifts at the eleventh hour which may reduce your estate taxes upon your death.

DID YOU KNOW THIS FACT: Retirement benefits, like life insurance, are generally not affected by your will. Instead they are affected by your beneficiary designations, and, if there is a primary and contingent beneficiary named, will not pass through probate. Moreover, if such assets do not pass through probate they usually will not be subject to claims of creditors. For example, if Richard had died in that car accident where he was at fault, and his retirement account was payable to his estate, the driver of the other car could sue and collect that money to satisfy any judgment they received against Richard in excess of his liability coverage under this automobile policy. This problem usually arises after the first or primary beneficiary is dead; accordingly, even if your spouse is your primary beneficiary, you should name a contingent beneficiary in the event that you and your primary beneficiary pass away together.

OPINION: Retirement accounts provide an excellent and unique opportunity to minimize taxes (estate and income) on these benefits through the proper beneficiary designations and proper planning. These matters need to be carefully coordinated with the provisions of the will and the Living Trust. Careful planning here can often save thousands, if not hundred of thousands, of dollars.

THE YOUNG EXECUTIVE WHO WAS TOO BUSY AND THE EIGHTEEN-YEAR-OLD PROBLEM

A young couple in their mid-thirties had two small children. The husband owned a fifty percent interest in a small business that he and a friend had formed. The wife was a stay at home mom. The husband died instantly in a car accident. Fortunately, the business had a $1,000,000 life insurance policy to purchase the husband's interest in the company. However, this $1,000,000 benefit was paid into the husband's estate. Like many young people, the husband had never executed a will or Living Trust; he was too busy. As a result, his estate had to go through probate and his assets passed to his heirs under the intestacy statute—the statute that applies if you die without a will.

If the husband had drafted an estate plan, he most likely would have left his estate to his wife. Under the intestacy statute at that time, his wife only received the first $60,000 plus one-half of the excess. The balance was split between the two very young children who each had to have a conservator appointed to invest and monitor the approximate $200,000 given to each child. The wife had no right to that $400,000, which passed by statute to the children. Each year the conservator had to file an annual accounting for the use of the money for the benefit of the children. Because the children were so young at the time, their estates were likely to become substantial by the time they reached 18. Under state law, that money, even if it has then reached $1,000,000, goes directly to the child, outright, on his or her 18th birthday. There is no question that if the husband had given any thought to the consequences of dying without a will and trust, he would have planned for a much different result. Unfortunately, he no longer had any say.

DID YOU KNOW THIS FACT: In most states, minors are considered adults at age 18 and, therefore, are entitled to receive their gifts outright at that age. A large sum of money in any 18-year-old's hands can be very dangerous, to say the least. One of the biggest benefits of a Living Trust is the ability to delay and stagger distributions of money until the beneficiaries have matured to the point where they can handle monetary responsibilities. For example, a Living Trust can be set up so beneficiaries receive their inheritances over time—say one third each at ages 25, 30 and 35. It can also provide the Trustee with the discretion to make payments to the beneficiary prior to that time for certain worthwhile purposes (such as college costs, buying a home or medical expenses). The Trustee can invest the rest of the money until the beneficiary (for example, the child or grandchild) can properly handle the money.

These Trust provisions correct a common estate planning mistake: people who leave their assets outright to their children (who may be adults), but, if a child is not alive at the time of a parent's death, the assets go to that child's children (i.e. the grandchildren), who may be minors or perhaps, even worse, young adults who are not capable of managing the money they may inherit. Living Trusts are the most common and cost-effective means of planning for these contingencies.

THE GREEDY KIDS—
AND YOU DIDN'T THINK YOU HAD ANY

The death of a family member often brings out the worst in people. Here is but one example. An elderly man with ten children and a modest estate decided that the easiest way to handle his affairs was to put his home in joint ownership with one son and his bank accounts in joint ownership with another son, with the "understanding" that they would split those assets with their siblings after his death. He also executed a will, which indicated those were his wishes. Unfortunately, greed overtook the two sons who were more interested in keeping the assets for themselves. Amazingly, after the father died, the two brothers refused to share even their father's personal property with their brothers and sisters. Because the estate was so modest and there were so many children, it was not financially or emotionally worthwhile for the "disinherited" siblings to take their brothers to task. However, the former family unity was totally destroyed, a tragic situation that might have been avoided if the father had managed his affairs differently.

THE DIVORCED MOTHER AND THE
18-YEAR-OLD PROBLEM

A female attorney, a single parent with a 12-year-old daughter, contracted a terminal illness. Although she contacted an attorney to draft a will and trust after she became ill, she never executed it. Her daughter, by state law, was the sole heir of her estate, as her mother had wanted, but the terms of that inheritance were certainly not. Under state law, the estate (approximately $400,000) went through probate. It was then transferred into a conservatorship established for the daughter. The daughter went to live with her father, the ex-husband of the woman, in another state. The conservator, who was not the father, filed an annual accounting with the court every year, with his fees paid out of the conservatorship. The daughter, who was now living with and being influenced by her father, had the right to receive the money outright at age 18. The daughter's estate grew to over $600,000 by the time she turned 18. The father, who had a terrible track record for investments, attempted to influence the daughter about what to do with the money. The daughter elected to keep the money with the third-party conservator, creating many hard feelings.

DID YOU KNOW THIS FACT: A Living Trust—with a Trustee hand-picked by the mother—would have avoided this entire situation, which came within an eyelash of being a total disaster. Again, a Living Trust gives you the power to control who will receive your money when you die and also gives you the power to choose the person who will watch over your money.

To make matters worse, had the daughter died without a will after turning 18, all of the mother's money would have gone to her ex-husband—an unforeseeable and appalling result. By staggering distributions in a Living Trust and picking a contingent beneficiary of her choice, the mother could have easily avoided this possible outcome.

OPINION: A good Living Trust will contain a contingency or disaster clause that specifies where your money should go if your immediate family is dead. Usually brothers and sisters or charities are the beneficiaries. Moreover, without a "disaster clause" the money can go to the State—a terrible result for most people.

Many estate plans never address this issue. The consequence can be a disaster. For example, a single mom set up a trust for her son, which provided that if the son was also dead the money was to be divided as if she had died without a will—i.e. as provided in the intestacy statutes. Those statutes stated that the money should be divided equally between her parents. The problem was that she was estranged from her father. Unfortunately, when she died in an accident with her son, her father ended up with one-half of the money. The devil is always in the details so make sure your estate planning lawyer is competent and covers these issues.

FUNDING MAKES THE LIVING TRUST
WORK PROPERLY

An elderly man became very sick from cancer and was about to die. He had two children who did not get along. Unfortunately, he had an inexperienced lawyer draft his Living Trust; and for reasons that are still not clear, the Trust was never funded (i.e. many of the assets were never placed into the Trust). As a consequence, he still personally owned many of his assets at his death. Those assets now had to be probated (i.e. used to pay his debts, then the balance transferred to his Trust for distribution to his two children). By failing to properly fund the trust, the man did not achieve one of the biggest benefits of Living Trusts—avoiding probate.

DID YOU KNOW THIS FACT: After a Living Trust is established (i.e. the Trust Agreement is signed by you), you must put your assets into the Trust so that they will be distributed in accordance with your wishes when you die. You usually do this by transferring the assets from you, personally, to you as Trustee of your Trust. (Before you die, you still control them as you did before, except that, technically, you own them as Trustee of your Trust; you can sell them, buy them, exchange them, or give them away just like you did before. However, since you own the assets, as Trustee of the Trust and not personally, when you die, the assets avoid probate).

Your Living Trust only works on those assets that are put into the Trust; thus, if you do not put the assets into the Trust, the Living Trust will not work properly. Think of the Living Trust as a set of instructions, which you have given to the person you trust (the Successor Trustee) to use and with which to distribute your money after you die or become disabled. However, if you do not give the Successor Trustee any money with which to work, he can not do what you asked him to do. Thus, it is very important that your assets be put into the Trust and that the beneficiary designations are coordinated properly on the life insurance and assets. This process—called a "funding the Trust"—is as important as the Living Trust itself; without proper funding, the Living Trust is not worth the paper it is written on.

THE WRONG BENEFICIARY DESIGNATION

A young man was married with two young children. Prior to getting married, he had purchased a life insurance policy worth approximately $250,000. Like most young couples, their house, a little bit in savings, and this insurance policy were all they possessed. Unfortunately, the husband never took the time to change the beneficiary designation from his parents to his new wife (who his parents didn't particularly like). Consequently, when he died unexpectedly of a heart attack, his young wife was left with their two young children to raise, a half constructed home and no money.

DID YOU KNOW THIS FACT: You must make sure your beneficiary designations are coordinated with the rest of your estate plan. As previously indicated, a Living Trust is an excellent repository for the insurance proceeds.

The above case studies are similar to actual matters that we have handled over the years in the estate and financial services industries. They provide real world examples of how a Living Trust, when part of an overall estate plan, can provide you with a cost-effective and simple means to protect you and your family. As you can see from these case studies, a Living Trust also gives you freedom and independence. Now that you have seen the benefits in some real world examples, let's look at some of the technical aspects of a Living Trust.

V.

WHAT IS A LIVING TRUST— A MORE TECHNICAL APPROACH

DEFINITIONS AND TERMINOLOGY

As a practical matter, a Living Trust is a legal document that is used to transfer ownership of your assets to the people you love. As a technical matter, a Living Trust is a set of instructions that you give to another person, called a Trustee, who has the duty to care for your money when you die or become disabled. For example, you could give $20 to your brother and tell him to give it to your daughter if she goes to college after you are dead. In this case, your brother is the trustee who holds the money in trust for the benefit of your daughter, who is the beneficiary. You are the grantor or settlor, the person who sets up this trust relationship. If this arrangement (or instructions) is in writing, it is called a Trust Agreement.

Trust Agreements come in two basic forms: Testamentary Trusts and Living Trusts. Testamentary Trusts are trusts that only come into play when you are dead; they are usually included in your will and, therefore, you do not avoid probate with a testamentary trust. For that reason, they are not used very often anymore.

Living Trusts are created while you are alive. The term "Living Trust" is not a legal term at all; it is a layman's expression to describe what is legally called a "Revocable Inter Vivos Trust." Let's break down that phrase because it tells us a lot about the benefits of a Living Trust. The term "Revocable" means the Trust can be revoked or terminated; likewise, it can be changed or amended at any time up until your death. The flexibility to change any provision is one of the key benefits of a Living Trust—it allows you to deal with changes that occur during your life.

The term "Inter Vivos" means while you are alive. In other words, the Trust becomes effective while you are alive, rather than when you are dead, which is when a testamentary trust becomes effective.

That you create a Living Trust while you are alive often confuses people. They understand leaving money with one person in trust for another person, such as in the example above, but do not understand how that applies to them when they are alive. The answer is simple when you understand the players in the Living Trust.

THE LIVING TRUST PLAYERS

Let's briefly and informally review the Living Trust players:

Settlor. The Settlor is the person who sets up the trust relationship—hence the name "Settlor." The "Settlor" is sometimes is called the "Grantor"—the person who grants or gives the Trustee his power. As the Settlor, you control and establish the terms of your Trust. If you are married, you and your spouse may be Settlors of your own Trust or you may have a Joint Trust. The key is that you are in control.

Trustee. With almost every Living Trust, you are the Initial Trustee. Therefore, you make all the decisions regarding your Living Trust. You can sell any assets that you put into the Trust. You can change the investments after they are put into the Trust. And, you can put more assets into, or take assets out of, the Trust at any time. You keep control. But who do you want to look after your affairs when you die or become incapacitated? That's the Successor Trustee.

Successor Trustee. This is the person you trust to carry out your instructions and make decisions for you after you die or become disabled. He or she can be anyone you wish, as long as he or she is a responsible adult who is capable of acting on your behalf to fulfill your wishes upon your death or incapacity. In the event your chosen Successor Trustee either dies or is unable to serve in that capacity, he or she is replaced by another person of your choosing. That "pinch-hitter" is also called a "Successor Trustee."

If you are married, you and your spouse are typically Successor Trustees of each other's Trust. This way, either of you can automatically act for the other. If one of you becomes incompetent or dies, the Successor Trustee instantly has control of all Trust assets. And the court is excluded.

Beneficiaries. The person or persons who receive benefits under the Living Trust are called the "Beneficiaries." A key point often overlooked by people is that while you are alive, you (and your spouse if you are married) are typically the only beneficiaries. Thus, technically, you hold the assets in trust for your benefit and the benefit of your spouse—just like you did before. The only difference is that you hold the assets in the Trust. In a well-drafted Trust Agreement, if you become disabled, the Successor Trustee—usually your spouse—can use the Trust assets for your benefit, your spouse's benefit, and for the benefit of your children, particularly if they are minors. How else would they live if they could not reach these assets!!!???

Key Point. The key point of the Living Trust is that while you are alive, you are all three players in the Trust arrangement: you are the Settlor, the person who set up the Trust; the Trustee, the person who controls the money in the Trust; and the Beneficiary, the person who will receive the benefits under the Trust (along with your spouse and minor children).

Let's diagram the Trust relationship to show how it exists while you are alive:

Living Trust: Before You Die

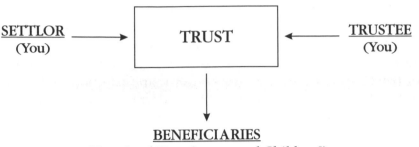

Now when you die, the other players in the equation change slightly. You are still the Settlor, the person who set up the Trust Agreement; in fact, no one can change it after you are dead. Since you are dead, you are no longer the Trustee; the person you selected to replace you, the Successor Trustee, takes your place. In addition, you are no longer a beneficiary of the Trust; instead, your wife and/or children (or other persons or charities you choose) are the beneficiaries. Moreover, you and no one else determines who gets the money, when, and under what terms. For example, you can withhold giving money to your children for any purpose other than education. You can make sure that sons-in-law do not receive any benefits. The key is that you have control.

Let's diagram the Trust relationship after you pass away:

Living Trust: After Your Death

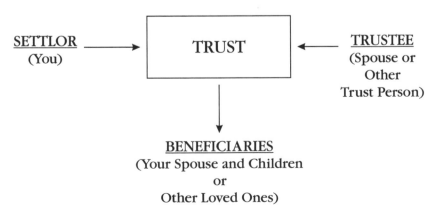

THE LAST PIECE OF THE PUZZLE: FUNDING

How does this allow you to avoid probate, you ask!!?? The answer lies in the last piece of the puzzle: putting the assets into the Trust. When you put assets into the Trust, you personally do not own the assets when you die; instead, you, as Trustee of your Trust, own the assets. Only assets that you own personally go through probate; the assets you own as Trustee (or in trust) stay in trust under the terms of the Trust Agreement, and the person you picked as Successor Trustee (often your spouse) takes over control of the assets. You avoid probate without giving up control.

The transfer of assets into the Trust is relatively simple: for example, to transfer a piece of property, you would generate a quit claim deed as follows: John Smith, a single man, quit claims to "John Smith, as Initial Trustee of the John Smith Living Trust U/A/D August 15, 2000, as may be amended or restated in the future."

Likewise the checking account would be changed to the "John Smith Living Trust U/A/D August 15, 2000, as the same may be amended or restated in the future."

A couple of technical notes. The term "U/A/D" means "Under Agreement Dated." The language referring to amendments and restatements is important to avoid any dispute that a beneficiary designation made payable to the Trust is still valid even if the Trust is later amended or restated. Believe it or not, people may challenge these transfers if they are not clearly spelled out. Of course, you are not around to tell anyone what you intended; accordingly, the care is warranted. Later in the book we will discuss funding of the trust in more detail.

As others have noted, it is helpful to think of the Trust as a box into which assets are deposited. You have the box on a string—meaning you can pull the box back and take assets out of it. Let's look at another diagram that shows how the assets are deposited into the Trust.

Funding Your Living Trust

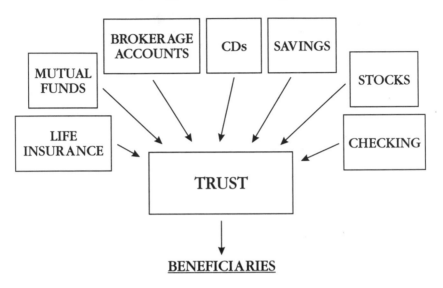

Remember: without funding, your Trust is not worth the paper it is written on!

VI.

<u>LIVING TRUSTS</u>
<u>ARE NOT JUST FOR THE RICH</u>

As you can see, a Living Trust is a simple, cost-effective way for ordinary people to protect what they own and transfer it to the people they love. Living Trusts have proven themselves to be the best tool for protecting your property—almost without regard to the size of your estate—and for protecting your freedom to make your own decisions concerning your own family and property!

That answer is important to you because of one word — FREE-DOM! A Living Trust gives you freedom to determine what happens to your property, both while you're alive and afterward. Although it's used by many people to save estate taxes (see Chapter IX), it is the most effective way for anyone, with an estate of any size, to maintain control.

The Living Trust is the same tool used by many famous people to keep their affairs private. In May of 1998, Frank Sinatra died. The world mourned, but the world was also curious about the Sinatra estate, which was estimated at $200 million. How much money did he leave to whom? We will never know the complete story. Here's what the Associated Press said:

Mr. Sinatra's attorney, Harvey Silbert, was quoted as saying, "...Sinatra's will covered only a portion of his wealth. The will really doesn't tell the story, he said. Mr. Sinatra, like most of us, had most of his assets in a Living Trust, and that is never public information. A Living Trust is similar to a will but is not subject to probate and therefore does not become a public document."

— *Michael White, Associated Press*

By putting his assets into a Living Trust, Mr. Sinatra was able to protect his own, and his family's, privacy and dignity. J. Paul Getty, H. L. Hunt, John D. Rockefeller, William Waldorf Astor, John F. Kennedy and many members of Congress have used the Living Trust as their estate planning tool of choice. But a Living Trust is not only for the rich. It's for any family that wants freedom and control of its own property. Computers and legal specialization in this area has made a Living Trust affordable for everyone. Moreover, your privacy and dignity is no less valuable than Mr. Sinatra's.

You can not be blind to the facts: in our country, approximately $6.8 trillion worth of assets is beginning to change hands from one generation to another. If you're middle age or older, and have accumulated any assets over the years, you're part of that process— whether you admit it or not. If you own assets (a house, land, pension plan, 401(k), CDs, a car, investments, jewelry, art), an important decision is placed squarely on your shoulders.

If you are like most Americans, you will spend 80,000 hours working to accumulate your wealth. Don't waste part of it by paying unnecessary estate taxes, probate fees, attorney and personal representative fees. You need the right tool to avoid paying these unnecessary taxes, expenses and fees.

The question is what tool are you going to use to protect your assets from taxes? What tool are you going to use to make sure your assets are distributed to your heirs in the manner you desire? What tool is not only cost-effective but will also accomplish all your objectives?

The right tool for the right job.

If you have ever tried to knock a tent peg into the ground with a rock, you know the value of using the right tool for the right job.

Protecting and controlling your property is a big job. It calls for the right tools. If you don't use the right tools for this job, the federal and state governments will certainly tax and probate your assets to the fullest extent possible. Even with the simplified probate procedures in some states, the cost of probate exceeds the cost of preparing a Living Trust.

Without the correct tool for your protection, your heirs will inherit only a portion of what they could have inherited. Without a flexible tool that gives you the freedom to control your property before and after you die, your family could suffer needlessly. That's the disturbing news.

The good news is that you can protect your assets right now. You can protect your family's inheritance right now.

When we talk with people about Living Trusts, the comments we hear most often are, "My parents had a will. If it was good enough for them, why would I need a Living Trust?"

Remember the phrase, "What you don't know might hurt you!" That's exactly the point. You see, in our parents' day, very few people had substantial assets. Their belongings consisted of a house, some furniture, a small bank account and a little jewelry. They did not have a retirement plan, CDs, a 401(k), an IRA or any investments. Many of our parents did not even have life insurance. Their last will and testament was an effective tool for that situation.

Those days are long gone. Today, our lives are much more complex. We have cars, a home, a fishing cabin in a different state, retirement plans, life insurance policies and investments. Over time, inflation has caused the value of our property to increase. We also have more complex families produced by divorces, with the complications of ex-spouses and stepchildren.

Since today's world is so much more complex, a will is usually not a cost-effective way to transfer assets to loved ones.

The most effective tool in nearly every estate planning situation is a Living Trust. Is a Living Trust right for you and your family? Probably. Read the rest of this book and then decide for yourself. We think you will agree with us.

©DG 1991

VII.

A DETAILED LOOK AT THE
MAJOR BENEFITS OF A LIVING TRUST

Most people think a will is all they need to pass on property and assets to their heirs. That may be true, but every will must pass through probate. Probate can be a dreadful and expensive experience for a typical family, even with the simplified procedures adopted in some states. One of the biggest benefits of a Living Trust is avoiding probate. This chapter examines that benefit and many others in detail.

1. Avoiding Probate

The word "probate" comes from the Latin word meaning "to prove." Probate is the means used to prove the validity of your will. It is initiated by having your will presented to the court, proving that it is your last will and testament. That's the first thing that separates a will from a Living Trust.

A will is part of the probate process, but a Living Trust usually avoids the probate process.

The probate process includes:

(a) Determining if the will is valid or legal. Since there are a number of laws and requirements that every will must meet, it is possible that even a good will can be held to be invalid. If a will is held to be invalid, then your property gets distributed under the intestate laws (intestate means to die without a will). The intestate laws are, basically, the state's best guess as to how you want your property distributed. Unfortunately, the state is often wrong. **(Note: someone who stands to inherit more under the intestate laws than from your will has a strong incentive to challenge your will and have it declared invalid).**

We are not alone in our concern about wills. In an address to the American College of Trial Lawyers, renowned trial attorney Leon Jaworski stated, "...a will is more apt to be the subject of litigation than any other legal instrument." – The Living Trust Revolution, Robert A. Esperti and Renno L. Peterson. The reason wills are contested so often, the authors explain, is that the typical probate process almost invites people to file objections to the will and claims against the estate.

According to Marshall Loeb, John Langbein, a Yale law professor, calls the probate process in some states "corrupt," meaning that the court fees are often outrageous and your assets might not be allocated in a manner that would have met your approval. Marshall Loeb, "Not Just for the Leisure Class: Trusts can be useful for Middle-Income Americans too," cbsmarketwatch.com July 26, 2000.

(b) Officially confirming the personal representative/executor named in the will or, if no representative is named, the court will select one of its own choosing.

(c) Notifying the court of the deceased person's death and informing all the people involved that probate has started. That usually includes all potential heirs whether named in the will or not, and sending notice to all potential creditors whether legitimate or not.

(d) Taking an inventory of all property and determining its value.

(e) Filing estate, inheritance and income tax returns and paying the deceased person's debts and taxes.

(f)   Preparing periodic and a final inventory or accounting to the court, which lists all assets and liabilities.

(g)   Distributing the remainder of the property to the heirs.

(h)   Closing the estate.

Probably the most important benefit of a Living Trust is that it allows you to avoid probate for the most part. If that were the only benefit, it would be well worth the effort for you to get one, even with today's simplified probate procedures in some states. However, that's not the only benefit. A Living Trust provides you and your family with an army of protection that is one of the most powerful tools in the world for retaining control of your property and minimizing the cost of passing your assets to the next generation.

An additional word is warranted on probate. Originally, a will was a private, intimate statement spoken by a person on his or her deathbed. The statement was usually delivered to a priest. From those earliest days, priests and witnesses realized that the dead rarely protest when you ignore their dying wishes.

History shows that it was the church, instead of the person's family, that received most of the property. As a result, laws were enacted which provided that a last will and testament was not valid unless it was witnessed by two or three people. As a result of efforts to control these abuses and others, the laws and regulations surrounding wills are highly technical.

Until recently, the complex nature of wills and probate has created an area of law filled with pitfalls and land mines. Recently, progressive states have adopted many procedures to simplify the probate process. In many respects, these new laws make probating an estate similar to having a Living Trust. However, while no empirical data exists at this point, most practitioners believe the new laws have not replaced the need for establishing a Living Trust; rather, the new laws will only make probate a little more tolerable for those who neglected, for whatever reason, to prepare a Living Trust.

2.   Cost

Going through probate can be expensive. The AARP estimates that three to eight percent of the typical estate will be lost to probate fees. Probate includes these fees: court costs, appraisal fees, attorney fees and executor or personal representative fees. Let's look at each one:

A.   Court costs

Court costs can range from a few hundred dollars to several thousand dollars. These include: filing fees, publication fees and inventory fees. Inventory fees, which are paid to the probate court, are based on a percentage of the assets going through the probate court. You have no control over these costs, unless you have a Living Trust.

B.   Appraisal fees

Probate attorneys need to learn the value of your property and other assets. This value is important for income and estate tax purposes, to calculate the inventory fees and to determine how much can be made available to pay creditors, the executor and the attorneys. Therefore, in many cases, an appraiser will need to be hired to place a value on certain assets.

C.   Attorney fees

In the probate process, attorneys fees, along with personal representative fees, may be the largest category of fees your family will have to pay.

Attorney fees are assessed on two different bases: "reasonable standard" and a percentage basis. In either case, an extraordinary fee can be requested for extraordinary services.

Under a reasonable standard, the attorney usually charges his normal hourly rate, which typically ranges from $125 to $350 per hour and the Court then determines whether the total charges are reasonable for the work that was performed. A hearing is then held to approve the fees unless all beneficiaries agree the fees are reasonable.

The other method of approving fees is the percentage method. Under the percentage fee method, the attorney receives a fee based on a percentage of the value of your probate assets. The method for calculating the fee varies but, in most cases, the fee is based on your gross estate without reducing it for any liabilities you may owe. Fees under the percentage method can be very high and not related to the difficulty of the work performed.

In all states, extraordinary fees are granted entirely at the discretion of the probate court. Extraordinary services may include the following: (a) managing your business; (b) selling property in a complicated transaction; (c) preparation of estate, inheritance, income, sales or other tax returns; (d) handling litigation or contests claims against your estate; (e) filing suit to collect assets or defending a contest to the will.

D. Personal Representative and Executor fees

In general, fees paid to the personal representative (also called an executor) who probates your estate can run into thousands of dollars. Personal representative fees, like attorney fees, are usually based on the reasonable standard or the percentage basis. Again, extraordinary fees can be requested.

In contrast, the fees for setting up an estate plan with a Living Trust are usually substantially less than the cost of probating your will and transferring assets. The fees charged for preparing the documents for a Living Trust are typically a set fee for most routine estate plans; extremely complicated estate plans are still prepared on an hourly rate basis.

As previously discussed, the process of transferring title of your assets into your Living Trust is called "funding." For the most part, the cost of funding a Living Trust is virtually non-existent. For example, the bank that has your checking, savings and CDs will re-register those accounts for you. The stockbroker will re-register those accounts for you. The insurance agent will help you change the beneficiary or re-register your life insurance and investment products. There may be a minor amount of legal fees for drafting deeds or transferring stock in privately held companies to a Living Trust, but again, these costs are almost always nominal when compared to probating the same estate.

Please note that both the personal representative and the attorney will charge for their time to transfer these assets when you go through a typical probate. Thus, one of the biggest savings of money (and time) is that you handle the re-registering of your assets, at a nominal expense while you are alive. There may be minor costs associated with transferring the assets upon death, but since you have done most of the legwork, these expenses are minimized.

3.   Protects you in Disability or Incapacity.

If you become disabled, you could be ruled "incapacitated" by the court. In that case, you will lose control of your power and freedom to make legal decisions. A Guardian and Conservator will be appointed for you—a person who you did not select will handle your affairs and file annual reports with the Court. To protect yourself and your family from that situation, act now and execute a Living Trust, a Durable Power of Attorney and a Healthcare Power of Attorney. Without those documents, a Guardian and Conservator may have to be appointed by the Probate Court—an expense that can be easily avoided. Moreover, you have the choice of whom will handle your affairs—instead of some Probate Judge who does not know your feelings—since you can no longer express them.

If the court declares you incapacitated, it can be a painful process for your family to endure. In real life, Groucho Marx experienced that very situation. The court declared him incompetent, and subsequently, there was a huge battle for control over his care and his money. Tragically, it was the end of his life that was the biggest joke, as the battle for control was reported all over the world. A Living Trust, together with a Durable Power of Attorney and Medical Power of Attorney, could have prevented that circus.

4.   Maximum Privacy and Dignity

Probate can be time-consuming, inconvenient and expensive. It can be an unpleasant, emotionally trying experience. Most important, you must recognize that while you won't go through it, your family will.

Many probate transactions are a matter of public record. Your will (like all wills) must go through probate. Personal information about you and your family may be open to the general public. However, if you've transferred your assets to a Living Trust, your personal information should be shielded from the general public. That's because the assets in your Living Trust do not go through probate. **Remember that that is exactly what Sinatra and Kennedy did to maintain privacy. You deserve the same.**

If you're a business owner, you don't need this public exposure. We are certain that you don't want your financial records known to the world. Even if you're not a businessperson, when you go through probate, people may be able to find out how much your estate is worth, as well as how much money your heirs inherited. We seriously doubt that you'd want that information made public.

5.   Easier for Your Family

To probate a complex estate with multiple bank accounts, retirement plans, investments and homes takes a long time and is very expensive. When setting up a Living Trust you effectively eliminate most costs by taking care of these matters yourself while you are alive.

Obviously, the time when your family is grieving over you is the worst time for them to be bothered with legal problems or doctors asking about life support systems and organ donations. Don't put your family through those agonizing decisions. Don't force them to guess what your wishes would have been.

The effort you put into organizing your affairs with your Living Trust will make it easier for your assets, documents and instructions to be handled later. Organizing your affairs and setting up a Living Trust will make living much easier for your loved ones.

Getting organized with a Living Trust and arranging for all your assets to flow through your Living Trust will provide the assistance and peace of mind your family will need when you die.

Most of you raised your children with the kind of values that encourage always trying to do the right thing. Getting your own affairs in order with a Living Trust is not only the right thing to do, the sense of relief and accomplishment you will experience will be tremendous.

6. Control: Part I

As a result of the probate process, when people die, their wishes may be ignored and loved ones disinherited. The probate court has direct and indirect control over the entire process. If there is anything wrong with your will, the judge can throw it out and say you died without a legal will, or that you died "intestate." As we discussed, if that happens, the property is distributed under a statute adopted by the state legislature. If none of your family or heirs is still alive, your assets usually go to the state. If you don't have a will or Living Trust, the state legislature will determine who gets your property.

However, don't blame the Probate Judge; he is just doing his job. You made the big mistake by allowing your private affairs to be handled by a Judge. When put in that position, the Probate

Judge will do his or her best to rule correctly, rest assured, but why let a Judge control your affairs in the first place.

Consequently, the probate process, not you or your family, has ultimate control over how your will is interpreted. Families are typically accustomed to handling their affairs privately and independently. Suddenly losing that control can be very frustrating and lead to results you may not have intended. Paying for it can be expensive, to say the least.

Rest assured, however, that no Probate Judge throws out wills lightly. However, unfortunately, there are often ambiguities in wills that require interpretation. Planning for the distribution of assets if one of your children predeceases you is a common situation that needs to be addressed clearly. To avoid costly probate battles over interpretation of ambiguous documents is but only one reason for having an experienced estate planning lawyer.

Here's one quick example that happens all the time. A Probate Judge, no matter how well intentioned, can rarely, if ever, fix the following:

Dad establishes a joint account for $10,000 with oldest daughter (put in by dad). It is designed to cover expenses, while dad is alive, in the event he can no longer handle his own affairs. Dad gets sick and his conscientious daughter takes care of him for two years before he dies. Dad's will says that everything is split 50-50 between daughter and her brother who lives out of state and only sees Dad every other year.

Who gets the money? Answer: Daughter. Reason: Because, as a general rule, joint accounts go to survivor. Son thinks dad wanted to split the money 50-50 but he will probably lose because the law requires him to submit evidence to show that Dad wanted a 50-50 split between his children for that account. There is no real evidence to help him. The will doesn't apply to joint accounts. Dad is dead and, therefore, is not talking about his intentions. The daughter will not roll over and "tell the truth" in her deposition, taken at $250 per hour by the lawyers. Moreover, can the son really afford to hire a lawyer to fight over $10,000, particularly with his slim chances of winning?

In contrast, when you transfer your assets to your Living Trust, you don't have those problems because you don't lose control. A Trust is not a person; it does not get sick, die, marry, divorce, remarry or go bankrupt. Regardless of what happens to the people who travel through your life, you maintain control over what happens to the assets in your Living Trust. That includes what the assets are, who gets them, when they're distributed, by whom, and in what amount.

7. Control Part II: Who Receives What (Assets)... and When, and You Cover Contingencies

As we previously discussed, a Living Trust is like a big box: all the money goes into one central pot and then is distributed to the beneficiaries.

Moreover, with a Living Trust you can really retain control of your assets after you're gone—controlling those assets from the grave, so to speak. One of the most powerful benefits of a Living Trust is that you control when your beneficiaries receive their inheritances. Assets can be distributed immediately, or they can remain in the Trust until your beneficiaries reach the age(s) you want them to inherit. It could be 25, 30, 35 or on a wedding day — the decision is yours.

That could be extremely important if the beneficiary is a teenager. That college fund could turn into a summer full of parties or shopping if the money were to be paid to the teenager at age 18.

A Living Trust also allows you to cover contingencies. For example, if one of your sons dies before receiving all of his inheritance, that money could be put into trust for his children (your grandchildren) and then distributed when they reach the proper age. Moreover, for a person who only has one child, a revocable trust can cover the contingency of that person dying and leaving no children. Do you want that money to go to your church or to another source? A well-thought out Living Trust covers these types of contingencies.

A perfect example of dealing with contingencies is the trust set up by the Kennedys for their children. The Kennedy family has suffered personal tragedy beyond belief, but Joseph Kennedy's estate plan has covered these contingencies and still provides benefits for his great grandchildren today—long after his death. With proper planning, you too can control your money from the grave — which is only fair since it is your money.

You can also provide for the care of a loved one with special needs. And, you can keep assets in the Trust to take care of newborns, even unborn descendants and future generations to come.

8. Flexible and Can Be Changed at Any Time

Your Living Trust is flexible enough to grow and change with you throughout your lifetime. As your family situation and goals change through births, deaths, relocations, illnesses and divorces, you can address the projected needs within your Living Trust.

You might also want to change the Trustee or Successor Trustee or add a beneficiary. You don't need to completely rearrange your Trust to accommodate changes in your life. You simply need to add an amendment.

You can remove assets from your Living Trust and you can add new ones. You can even terminate your Trust. Remember, part of the technical definition of Living Trust is the word "revocable," and that means it can be changed or terminated.

9. Can Reduce Estate Taxes

Besides avoiding probate, a Living Trust can help you to significantly reduce estate taxes. This topic is discussed in detail in Chapter IX. Suffice it to say that if you and your spouse have substantial assets (say, in excess of $675,000), certain types of Living Trusts can be adapted to save estate taxes. In making this calculation, be sure to include all of your real estate, investments and life insurance.

10. Recognized in all States

If you have a will, it may not be recognized in other states, particularly as it relates to real estate located in a state other than the state of your residence. The reason for this is complicated but, basically, whenever one moves from one state to another, it is advisable to have a new will executed because the requirements for a valid will are similar, but not identical, from one state to another. Therefore, the will may no longer be valid in the new state.

In contrast, a Living Trust is usually recognized in every state; as a consequence, even if you move to another state, your Living Trust will be effective. Moreover, if you own a vacation home in a second state, a Living Trust will pay for itself because you avoid ancillary probate in the state in which you are not a resident.

11. Avoids Ancillary Probate

Stop for a moment and think of all the negative experiences probate might bring to your family: costs, inconvenience, and possibly trauma and loss of control. Now, multiply that by the number of states in which you own property. Not a pretty picture.

If you own property in different states and attempt to protect your estate with a will, your estate will probably be probated in each state! And, you'd probably have to hire a new attorney in each state.

Example. Let's paint another picture of how this process could produce a very negative outcome. Imagine your daughter marries a boy from another state. The couple decides to settle in the boy's hometown. As a wedding present, you buy a lovely little home for them. Until the marriage stands the test of time, you keep it in your name.

If you die before transferring ownership to them, your estate will probably be probated in the other state, as well as in your home state. Your family would pay for two attorneys and two probates.

One Living Trust eliminates the situation above. A Living Trust can control all your assets, even real estate you may own in other states. So if you have a Living Trust, and you have transferred title of your important assets into it (especially those assets in other states), there is usually no need for additional probates in other states when you die.

Note, however, you should consult with an experienced estate planning attorney. In some states, real estate owned jointly by husband and wife have a special exemption from claims of creditors that may be lost if the real estate is transferred to the Living Trust.

12. Shorten The Time Frame for Distributions

The probate process may take a few months; however, some take as long as several years to complete. The average probate takes about 15 months. In complex situations it is not unusual for probate to last 18 months to three years. Some probate cases have gone on for many years.

The reason probate can be so prolonged is related to the substantial amount of activity required to process an estate through probate. As previously discussed, probate involves several separate steps that each take time such as (a) gathering material and filing a petition; (b) publishing notice to creditors; (c) taking inventory of all assets and obtaining appraisals (if necessary); (d) paying claims of creditors after publishing notice; (e) preparing an accounting of assets and expenditures and filing petitions for distribution and accounting; and (f) closing the file (see discussion above). For most persons with simpler estates, a Living Trust may make these activities unnecessary and shorten the time for distribution of assets to the beneficiaries.

13. Minimizes Emotional Stress

With the court supervision of your estate removed, your family can continue its normal day-to-day routines more quickly and easily. Your affairs can be handled more efficiently and privately by the people you have chosen. Your family will be able to express their grief, each say their personal good-byes, and move on with their lives. If they have to endure a lengthy probate, their most lasting memory might not be of you. Instead, they may only remember lengthy and heartless court proceedings which could have been avoided.

14. Prevents Unintentional Disinheriting

With a Living Trust, you don't have to worry about unintentionally disinheriting anyone. As previously discussed, unintentional disinheriting can happen any time you give an asset to someone with the understanding that the asset is to be passed on to someone else, which is a very bad idea. The "messenger" could keep the asset, sell the asset, give it to someone else or lose it to a creditor or spouse. As discussed earlier, this situation happens all the time and rarely do the people who get cheated have any recourse.

The better alternative is to put those assets into a Living Trust. The instructions in your Trust must be followed, so there is no risk that your wishes will not be followed.

15. Avoids the Problems of Joint Tenancy

Similar to the unintentional disinheriting problem, the joint tenancy problems are avoided with a Living Trust. As discussed in the case studies, a joint tenancy creates a number of problems including: (a) a loss of control by the true owner; (b) gift taxes caused by transfers to nominal joint tenants; (c) immediate probate of the assets if both joint tenants die together; (d) delayed probate after the death of one joint tenant if nothing further is done; (e) subjects the assets to the potential claims of creditors of the "nominal" owner; (f) creating the ability of the "nominal" owner to misappropriate your funds. The drug addict daughter—a real life case—should be enough to convince anyone of the risks of joint tenancy—risks which can be easily avoided with a Living Trust.

16. Generally More Difficult to Contest.

To invalidate a will, a person must generally prove that the will was not properly executed, that it was signed under duress, that it was signed under influence or that you were incompetent on the day it was signed. Those accusations are difficult to prove, but challenges like these are made in the courts every day. As a practical matter, trusts are generally more difficult to contest than a traditional will. A Living Trust does not generally "go public." It remains a private document. As a result, outsiders generally do not find out about your financial situation.

17. No Special Government Forms Required

As long as you are a Trustee of your Living Trust, you do not need a separate tax identification number, and you do not need to file a separate tax return. You continue to use your social security number and file the same personal income tax returns as you always have in the past.

After your death, the Successor Trustee will apply for a tax identification number and file a separate tax return for the Trust. Your attorney and/or CPA should be able to provide assistance if necessary.

18. Creditor Protection

Living Trusts do provide some measure of protection from creditors; however, fleecing creditors should never be the primary motivation for establishing a Living Trust. The benefit of a Living Trust vis-a-vis creditor protection is that certain assets made payable directly to the Living Trust (as compared with your estate) are not liable for the claims of creditors.

A word of background. Many states, including Michigan, provide that a Living Trust is secondarily liable for the claims against your probate estate. In plain English, that means that if your probate estate does not have enough assets to pay your administrative expenses, taxes and debts, the assets in your Living Trust will be used to pay such obligations.

However, not all assets in your Living Trust can be used to pay those creditors. The key exception is life insurance made payable to your Living Trust. Creditors should not be able to reach those proceeds to pay your debts in most states. Likewise, many states statutorily exempt certain retirement benefits for the payment of such claims and obligations. Such retirement benefits include amounts payable under a pension and profit sharing plan, IRA, 401(k), tax sheltered annuity (403(b)) and other retirement benefits under the Internal Revenue Code. In summary, the creditor protection offered by a Living Trust is superior to the creditor protection offered by a will.

VIII.

<u>LIVING TRUSTS AND THE REST OF THE ESTATE PLANNING TEAM</u>

As we have discussed, a Living Trust is the key component of your estate plan. It is like the quarterback on a football team; it tells everyone where to go on "go"—namely, who is going to receive money and under what conditions. However, just like a football team, other supporting players have an important role in your well being. A quarterback can not complete a pass to a wide receiver unless he has linemen to block for him and a receiver to catch the ball. Likewise, a Living Trust can not solve all of your estate planning problems alone. Here are the other members of the estate planning team.

1.   The Living Trust. As we discussed, the Living Trust is the key player; it controls who gets your money and when. It specifies who will handle your affairs after you are dead or disabled (the Successor Trustee). The Living Trust is a document that contains this information and more.

As you may recall, the Living Trust is the box into which moncy and other property must be placed for the Trustee, to be distributed according to your instructions. To deposit the money and other property into the Trust, a number of documents need to be executed to transfer the assets into the Trust. Several of these documents are discussed next.

2.   The Pour Over Will.   This is a legal document that acts as a "catch-all" for titled/registered assets and property you might have forgotten to place in your Living Trust. These properties may include the following: homes, land, vehicles, investments and other personal property. At your death, the Pour Over Will effectively transfers to your Living Trust any property not previously placed in the Trust. Graphically, this transfer is depicted as follows:

Pour Over Will

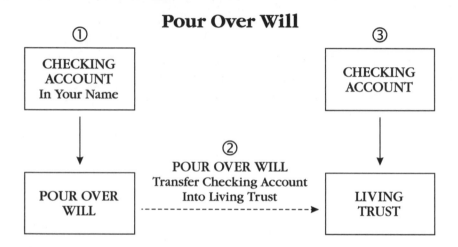

There are two things to remember about a Pour Over Will. First, remember, every will goes through probate. Items transferred with the Pour Over Will have to go through probate and then be transferred to the Trust. As discussed previously, this approach is usually not the most cost-effective way to transfer your assets and should only be used as a safety net in case some assets are not transferred into the Trust while you are alive. Second, the Trust must be designated as the beneficiary of the Pour Over Will.

Every competent estate planning lawyer will include a Pour Over Will in your estate plan. Given that you have a Living Will, you may ask why. There are several reasons. First, even with a Living Will, there may be assets that you forgot to put into the Living Trust after it was established; for example, you could buy a mutual fund in your name instead of in the name of your Trust. Second, there may be particular assets that you do not want to put into the Trust for a variety of reasons. For example, while cars can be placed into Trusts, it is rarely done, for several reasons. Auto insurance companies have a hard time with this concept, and in most states there is a simplified procedure for transferring cars upon death. Third, in some states the will (not the Living Trust) has to specify which assets would be primarily liable for taxes. Fourth, in most states, you can add a simple handwritten Memo-randum, referenced in your will, that specifies who will receive your personal effects.

3. Personal Effects Memorandum.   Some states allow you to prepare a simple memorandum that specifies who will get certain items of tangible property (e.g., "I leave my watch to my daughter, Sara, and my wedding ring to my other daughter, Sally.") Just imagine the hurt feelings and arguments this simple document can prevent.

This memorandum can usually be handwritten and can be updated as often as you want without having to go back to your lawyer for every little change. A good practice is to allow such a memorandum to be created under the Trust as well, since the personal property is usually transferred to the Living Trust under the General Assignment, which is discussed below.

4.   General Assignment.   A General Assignment is a simple one-page document that transfers or assigns all items of personal property that are not titled to your Living Trust. You do not have to list each specific item of personal property, such as silverware, plates, furniture or hunting equipment. With this document, all of your personal property is automatically included and will be distributed to the beneficiaries you named in the Trust. For that reason, a Living Trust should usually allow you to make a Personal Effects Memorandum, which serves under the will as well.

5.   Beneficiary Designations.   Beneficiary designations need to be executed for assets such as life insurance, annuities and similar assets. Normally, these assets will be made payable to "the then acting Trustees under the Living Trust of [Your Name] u/a/d August 15, 2000, as may be amended or restated from time to time."

Care should be exercised before making your Living Trust the primary beneficiary of your retirement plans such as a 401(k), TSA/403(b) and IRA. There are situations where the proper beneficiary designation can greatly reduce estate and income taxes on the distributions from these plans. A Living Trust can be named as a beneficiary, but the Living Trust must satisfy several conditions to qualify for this special treatment. Moreover, for many people, naming the surviving spouse as the primary beneficiary allows the surviving spouse to put the IRA 401(k) or other retirement account in her or his name, thereby allowing a deferral and/or reduction of taxes upon receiving distributions. A detailed discussion of this topic is beyond the scope of this book, but you should see an estate planning attorney for further guidance on this all-important topic.

6.   Documents Retitling Assets.   You will need to retitle most of your assets into the name of the Trust from your own name. For example, from "Bob Jones" to "Bob Jones, as initial Trustee of the Bob Jones Trust . . . ." Retitling applies to savings and checking accounts, investment accounts, mutual funds and brokerage accounts.

Deeds for transferring real estate also need to be prepared; however, before you put your home into a Living Trust, you should consult with your lawyer. In some states, a house (and perhaps other real property) owned by a husband and wife together as "tenants by the entireties" (a/k/a husband and wife) are exempt from the claims of creditors and that special exemption may be lost if the property is put into the Living Trust. The loss of this exemption may not be important if you have adequate insurance, but again this issue should be discussed with a competent estate planning lawyer.

7. Certificate of Trust Existence. Sometimes called an "Abstract of Trust," this document either contains a copy of part of the Living Trust (without copying the parts that tell who gets what and when) or gives very brief descriptions of the contents of your Living Trust. The Trust Certificate usually contains other pertinent information and identifies all the Trustees and Successor Trustees. This document is important because it shows that the Trust exists without giving the full details of its provisions. For example, it can be given to financial institutions to prove the existence of the Trust while keeping the terms and conditions private.

8. Durable Power of Attorney. This document is important. It authorizes someone of your choosing (technically called an agent) to act for you with respect to financial matters under certain conditions, for instance if you become incapacitated, go into a coma or are confined to a nursing home. Usually, you name your spouse as the primary agent, and a child or other trusted person as the contingent agent. This person can only act as your fiduciary—which means that the person can not use the assets for their own benefit—only yours.

Let's say the condition of your health is declining, so you place your son's name on your checking accounts. Your thinking is, if an emergency arises, he'd have access to the money needed for medical bills as well as for regular home utility bills. That's a bad decision for two reasons:

• If he is sued, his creditors may be able to reach the money in those accounts. A simple traffic accident could bring about that situation.

• If your son gets divorced, his ex-wife could make a claim for a percentage of the money in the account.

The reason those situations can arise has to do with ownership. Any person whose name appears on a joint account is presumed by law to own the account as well, unless it is proven otherwise, which is complicated and expensive. Another person (a spouse, ex-wife or creditor) who has a right to your son's assets may also have a right to your account.

A Durable Power of Attorney, along with a Living Trust, solves that problem because the person can only use your money for your benefit if they do not own it.

A note on Durable Powers of Attorney. Some become effective only if a person is determined to be disabled by a doctor or doctors; others are immediately effective upon one's disability. At first blush, the first kind seems preferable because who would want someone to act for them unless they were disabled. Unfortunately, the reality in this day and age is that many doctors will not render an opinion that someone is disabled for fear of getting sued—those damn lawyers. Therefore, when you need your Durable Power of Attorney the most, you can not get anyone to certify that you are disabled. For that reason, it is often preferable to have the Durable Power of Attorney be effective immediately and to just be certain that the person holding the power is someone you trust.

Two further notes on Durable Powers of Attorney. Make sure they're in "recordable form," which means they can be recorded in the Register of Deeds office. For example, you may need to use a Durable Power of Attorney to execute and record a deed. Moreover, make sure that your signature on the Durable Power of Attorney is "Signature Guaranteed" by a financial institution such as a bank. A "Signature Guarantee" is a statement by the financial institution that the signature on the Durable Power is your signature. Without a Signature Guarantee, most brokerage houses, banks and other financial institutions will not recognize the Durable Power of Attorney. Of course, the Durable Power should have witnesses and be notarized.

9. Health Care Power of Attorney. A Health Care Power of Attorney ("HCPOA") is a power of attorney that is limited to medical decisions. It is usually authorized by state statute. The HCPOA is as much for your benefit as it is for your health care provider; in this day and age, they need to know who is the decision maker. Make sure you give a copy of the document to your primary care physician and hospital.

10. Living Will. A Living Will is used to state your wishes about whether to use, withhold or "unplug" any medical treatment if you become terminally ill. If you don't make these decisions when you're clear-headed, you will place your family under the incredible stress and anguish of deciding for you, if you become ill. In some states, a Living Will is not technically enforceable, but the doctor will usually recognize it as a practical matter in making the decisions concerning extreme care. Again, it is very important to deliver this document to your doctors well in advance of any illness. Without a Living Will, a doctor has to listen to a son or daughter—who may or may not have pure motives—tell him that "Mom would have wanted to die," when there is a small fortune in mom's account that will be spent if care is continued. Even if the child is right, it creates at least the appearance of possible foul play. Save everyone from this guesswork and heartache.

11. Anatomical Gift Declaration. Have you ever considered donating your organs when you die? With this simple document, you can donate your organs, thus saving a life or returning sight to a blind person. This document is where you do it, legally. In many states, all you have to do is complete a form when renewing your driver's license.

12. Nomination of Guardianship. This document is extremely important for people with minor dependents, dependents with special needs or people who don't have Durable Powers of Attorney. You use it to pre-determine and name (to the court) the person you want to take care of those special loved ones, in the event they are unable to care for themselves. In some states, this is covered as part of the will; in others, it can also be executed as a separate document. Please realize that selecting a guardian does not guarantee that the court will approve that person, but it greatly increases the likelihood that the person you selected will serve as guardian.

13. Organizational Document. This is an important document. It names the location of all your important papers. It is not always wise or recommended that you assemble all the actual documents in one place. If they're all in one place, they're all vulnerable to theft or destruction. Often, a better idea is to have a document that points to their locations.

You'd list items such as the location of the deed to your home, your safety deposit box, your original will, Living Trust, Durable Power of Attorney, life insurance policies, account statements, tax information, emergency medical information, adoption papers, divorce papers, prenuptial agreements and titles to vehicles. Without a doubt, when someone dies without having organized his or her documents, the one thing that is nearly always missing is the deed to the house. The other thing that many people lose is a life insurance policy. Don't force your family into the position of not being able to find a deed or life insurance policy that might be stashed in a box in the attic.

14. Personal Data Sheet. This is a biographical breakdown of your family members and personal friends. If you're a member of a civic, social or professional group, those people will want to know when you die. So, you'd want to list at least one contact person for each group, for instance: Rotary Club, Chamber of Commerce, Shriners, the bowling league, yacht club, volunteer fire department.

15. Consultants and Contacts. Like the Personal Data Sheet, this document links your family with business and professional people important to your life. These are your trusted advisors with whom your family will need to communicate after your death.

IX.

HOW TO USE LIVING TRUSTS
TO SAVE ESTATE TAXES

As you have seen, there are numerous reasons for setting up a Living Trust.   As you will notice, saving taxes is not even among them. However, for people with substantial assets, Living Trusts can be used to save a substantial amount of taxes. Here's how.

1.   Husband and Wife Are One.   When you got married, your vows stated that you and your spouse had become one. Believe it or not, the Federal Government believes that promise too. They treat the two of you as one person. As a result, when you leave everything to your spouse, no tax is paid. Graphically, the relationship looks like the following:

How Tax Laws Work

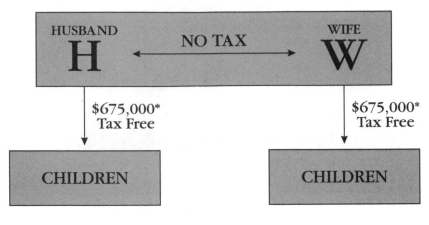

* in 2000

Please note the negative of this is also true. If you are not married, the special exemption for a spouse does not apply. Therefore, the only exemption you get is the exemption equivalent.

2. Leaving the Box and the Federal Tax. As you can see, as long as you stay inside the box of you and your spouse, the assets are not taxed. However, if you leave the box, and you have assets over a certain amount, your assets are heavily taxed. The amount of assets you can pass free of federal estate taxes to someone other than your spouse is called the exempt amount. (Note that, for the most part, we are going to be talking about federal estate taxes. Many states have inheritance taxes in addition, but those taxes are usually coordinated with the federal estate taxes. You should contact your local estate planning professional for details.)

In 1997, the federal government decided to gradually increase the amount of money that people could pass tax free to people other than their spouses. At the time, the exempt amount was $600,000. The increase in the exempt amount (as of 2000) is phased in as follows:

Year	Unified Credit Exemption Equivalent
1998	$625,000
1999	$650,000
2000	$675,000
2001	$675,000
2002	$700,000
2003	$700,000
2004	$850,000
2005	$950,000
2006	$1,000,000

A side note. The lawmakers sold the public on the graduated increase concept, telling them that the increase would provide additional relief to additional taxpayers because of the increase from $600,000 to $1,000,000. However, that is probably not true. If you had $600,000 in 1998 and you enjoyed an after tax return of 10% each year, and reinvested the proceeds, you would possess approximately $1,063,000 by the end of 2004 and $1,286,000 by the end of 2006. Accordingly, if you died in 2006, you pay taxes where you would not have had to pay taxes in 1998. This is hardly the tax savings for the average American that was represented to the public.

The federal estate tax is not a cheap date. It starts at 37% and increases to 55%. Here is a copy of the table.

2000 Estate & Gift Tax Table

Taxable Estate	Marginal Rate on Excess	Net Estate Tax
$675,000	37%	$0
$700,000	37%	$18,500
$750,000	39%	$37,000
$1,000,000	41%	$134,500
$1,250,000	43%	$237,000
$1,500,000	45%	$344,500
$1,750,000	45%	$457,000
$2,000,000	49%	$569,500
$2,250,000	49%	$692,000
$2,500,000	53%	$814,500
$3,000,000	55%	$1,079,500

Thus, if you are a widow and die with $1,500,000 in assets in 2000, all of which you gave to your children, you would owe $344,500 in federal estate taxes, plus inheritance taxes for your state of residence. There is a way to give more money to your family and keep it away from the IRS. But first you need two more pieces of information.

3.   Each of You Gets an Exempt Amount; Therefore, Twice as Much Can Pass Tax Free

As we discussed, each person has an exempt amount to pass to people outside the box of husband and wife. However, if dad leaves everything to mom, it passes tax free to mom, but dad wastes his exemption. (By the way, do not be offended by the references to dad dying first in our examples; based on actuarial studies, men, in fact, die younger than women do. In addition, women hold most of the wealth in the United States. Thus, our examples just track reality).

By wasting dad's exemption, you increase the taxes when mom dies by about $270,000. Let's put up some numbers here to see how this works. If dad and mom retain $1,350,000 in assets, dad dies in 2000, and leaves the entire amount to mom, no taxes are owed when dad dies. However, his exemption is wasted. When mom dies (let's assume she dies later in 2000), the entire amount above the exemption equivalent is subject to taxation. Thus, on the $1,350,000 amount going to the kids, mom will pay approximately $270,000, in taxes—money right out of the kids' pockets. Think how hard you worked for that money—what a shame. Let's look at how this works graphically:

All Money Left To Surviving Spouse

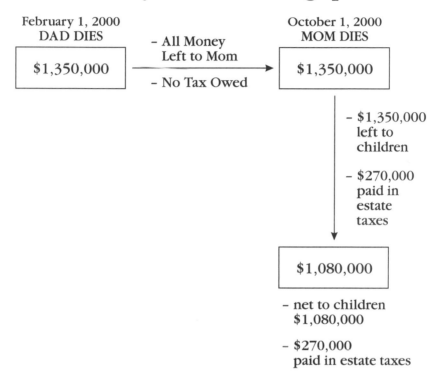

February 1, 2000
DAD DIES

$1,350,000

- All Money
  Left to Mom
- No Tax Owed

October 1, 2000
MOM DIES

$1,350,000

- $1,350,000
  left to
  children

- $270,000
  paid in
  estate
  taxes

$1,080,000

- net to children
  $1,080,000

- $270,000
  paid in estate taxes

However, this money doesn't have to be wasted. Instead, dad and mom could have divided the assets evenly between them and not paid any taxes. Thus, mom and dad would each own $675,000 in their own Living Trust. Dad's Trust provides that the entire amount goes to the kids upon his death. Mom has $675,000 in her Living Trust, and when she dies later in the year, that amount passes tax-free too. The result is that approximately $270,000 is saved in taxes. Let's see how that works as well.

Splitting Assets:
Leaving All Money to Children

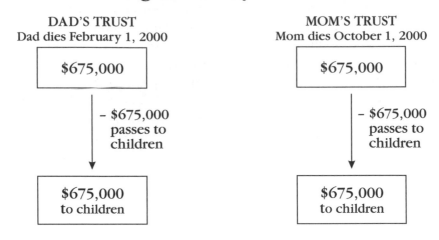

DAD'S TRUST
Dad dies February 1, 2000

$675,000

− $675,000
passes to
children

$675,000
to children

MOM'S TRUST
Mom dies October 1, 2000

$675,000

− $675,000
passes to
children

$675,000
to children

− $1,350,000 to children
− No federal estate taxes

However, that plan does not always work because $675,000 has gone to the kids while mom is alive. If Mom has substantial assets of her own, this plan would probably be okay. However, most husbands and wives want to take care of each other first, and if there is anything left over for the kids, that is great. With the money going outright to the kids, that money is gone and can no longer be used for mom's care. Is there a better way, where mom can have access to the money and still not waste dad's $675,000 exemption? (Note: remember this exemption increases to $1,000,000 by 2006.) The answer is yes. But first you need to know one more rule.

4. Dividing Up the Ownership Pie. Ownership of any property is a bundle of rights. Think of it as a piece of pie. You can divide up the pie and give some parts of it to your spouse without your spouse being considered the owner of the entire amount of the pie. In other words, we can put the $675,000 in a subtrust for the kids inside the Living Trust and give mom certain rights to get to or use the $675,000 without all of it being included in her estate, thereby wasting dad's exemption. This subtrust has many names: a "Bypass Trust," a "Credit Shelter Trust," and "Family Trust" among other names.

Remember we said that if you leave the $675,000 outright to mom, you waste dad's exemption because she owns that $675,000 when she dies. The federal tax code says you can give her certain rights without the $675,000 being treated as her property. How many rights are given to mom is a key part of a good estate planning lawyer's craft. For example, mom can have the right to receive income on the $675,000 and not be treated as owning the $675,000 itself. However, mom does not have the right to receive all of the $675,000 for any reason she desires. If she is allowed to access the money for any reason, the tax code regards her as the owner of the money because she has total control over it—technically called a general power of appointment. In that case, the $675,000 is included in mom's estate and dad's exemption is lost.

But, you can slightly limit that power and not waste dad's exemption. Mom can have the right to receive the principal for her health, support, maintenance and education—called an ascertainable standard—and still not be treated as owning the part of the $675,000 that she does not take out of the Family Trust. She can't, however, take the money out to buy a new house for her second husband. This power is called a limited power of appointment; because it is limited, mom is not treated as owning the money that she does not take out of the Trust.

Another way to limit this power is to allow another person or entity to make these decisions, for example, a bank. Because a bank exercises the control—and not mom—the power can be broader and the money will still not be included in mom's estate. Likewise, this power can be exercised jointly between mom and a third party—a bank or a daughter—but the third party has to have the power to decide if there is a disagreement. By giving this power to the third party, the property is not included in mom's estate.

Other rights can be given to mom without the assets of the Family Trust being included in mom's estate when she dies. The more rights she is given, the closer she moves toward "owning" the property without wasting dad's exemption. For example, mom can be given the right to take out of the Family Trust the greater of five percent of the assets of the Family Trust or $5,000 every year. Assuming there is $675,000 in the Trust, mom could take out $33,750 per year for no particular reason whatsoever. In addition, mom can be given the right to decide who among her children receives the remaining money of the Family Trust when she dies. This is called a limited power of appointment—you appoint or choose who gets the money among a limited group of people. Mom can't be given the power to choose anyone other than persons in the limited group or else it is a general power and the entire amount of the Family Trust is taxed in mom's estate. There are several other types of limited rights that mom can be given without wasting dad's exemption. All of these rights are driven by the tax code. Graphically, the ownership pie can be viewed as being divided up as follows:

Ownership Pie

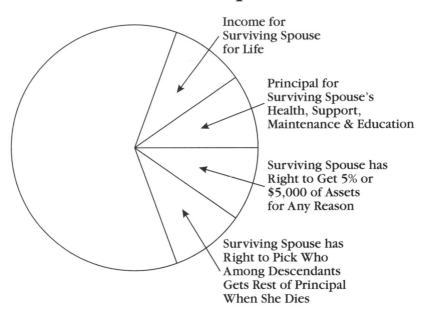

Income for
Surviving Spouse
for Life

Principal for
Surviving Spouse's
Health, Support,
Maintenance & Education

Surviving Spouse has
Right to Get 5% or
$5,000 of Assets
for Any Reason

Surviving Spouse has
Right to Pick Who
Among Descendants
Gets Rest of Principal
When She Dies

5. Review of the Major Principles. Before moving on, let's review the major principles:

a. There is an unlimited marital deduction; therefore all assets can be passed between spouses without federal estate taxes.

b. Each person can pass a certain amount of assets to persons other than your spouse without paying any taxes. This amount is $675,000 in 2000 and increases to $1,000,000 by 2006.

c. Leaving all assets to the other spouse wastes the exemption of the first spouse to die, thereby increasing taxes upon the death of the second spouse to die.

d. Leaving the exempt amount outright to people other than your spouse (such as your children) removes the assets from your spouse's estate, but deprives your surviving spouse of access or use of the assets.

e. The best solution (usually) is to transfer the amount of the exempt assets (currently $675,000, increasing to $1,000,000) into a Family Trust. The surviving spouse is then given a bundle of rights to use the assets without the assets being included in the surviving spouse's estate, therefore escaping taxation altogether.

Now, let's see how this works in the real world and with your Living Trust.

6. Back to the Living Trust. Let's pull this all together with a simple example. Suppose dad has $1,500,000 in various savings accounts, CDs, mutual funds and other investments. He sets up a Living Trust, and after reading this book, transfers ownership of the assets into the Trust (i.e. retitles the assets to himself as initial Trustee of his Living Trust). To save taxes, he creates a Family Trust with the balance of his assets being distributed outright to his wife upon his death. In plain English, the Living Trust says the following:

"When I die, divide my Living Trust assets into two parts. The first part is the Family Trust. The amount in the Family Trust will equal the amount that I can pass to my children free of federal estate taxes (i.e. $675,000). The rest gets distributed to mom outright. That amount would be $825,000 which equals $1,500,000 minus $675,000."

77

"Mom will get all of the income from the Family Trust. In addition, mom can take up to $5,000 or five percent of the Family Trust assets out for any reason whatsoever. [That is $33,750 per year] In addition, mom will have the right to use the principal (the $675,000 or whatever is left) for her health, support, maintenance and education. Finally, mom can designate among our children and grandchildren who will get what is left in the Trust. If she does not make any designation, then the remaining assets will be distributed equally among my children, but if one of my children has died before me, then that child's share will divided equally among his or her children (my grandchildren). That share will be held in trust and distributed for their benefit under separate Trusts for each of them."

Graphically, the assets are divided as follows:

Family Trust – Saving Taxes

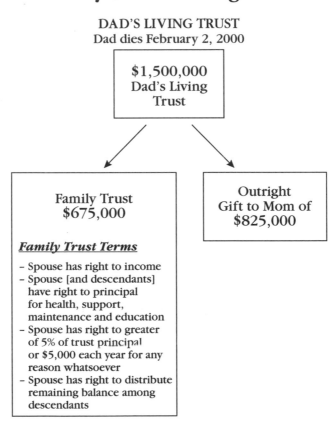

DAD'S LIVING TRUST
Dad dies February 2, 2000

$1,500,000
Dad's Living
Trust

Family Trust
$675,000

Family Trust Terms

– Spouse has right to income
– Spouse [and descendants]
  have right to principal
  for health, support,
  maintenance and education
– Spouse has right to greater
  of 5% of trust principal
  or $5,000 each year for any
  reason whatsoever
– Spouse has right to distribute
  remaining balance among
  descendants

Outright
Gift to Mom of
$825,000

Result: No Tax Owed Upon Death of Dad

At the time of dad's death, no estate tax is owed because the $675,000 is exempt from taxes (i.e. the exemption amount for gifts to people other than your spouse); the remaining $825,000 given outright to mom is also exempt from taxation because of the marital deduction. Remember, anything given by dad to mom and vice versa is exempt from taxation. Assume that mom dies a year later, and she still has the $825,000 at her death. Because she has a $675,000 exemption, she will only pay taxes on $150,000. As a result of using this approach, $1,350,000 passes tax free to the kids, saving approximately $270,000 in federal estate taxes.

There are other benefits to this approach. All the growth in the assets in the Family Trust passes estate tax free upon mom's death. For example, suppose mom lives for nine years and she does not need a lot of income from the Family Trust on which to live; in that case, the assets could be invested in growth assets that do not distribute dividends or other income. All of that growth passes free of federal estate tax to the kids. Assume the after-tax rate of return is eight percent per year. In that case, the $675,000 would grow to $1,350,000 for the kids in the Family Trust. That is in addition to the amount that mom holds, which is $825,000, plus the growth on that amount. Note: income taxes, of course, will need to be paid on the dividends and interest.

A Side note: the Rule of 72s. A handy rule of thumb to calculate growth of your assets is the rule of 72s. Take your after tax rate of return (say eight percent) and divide that number into 72 and that will tell you how long it will take to double your money. For example, if you had $100,000 and you received an eight percent after-tax rate of return, your money would double every nine years; 72 divided by eight is nine. Note that in nine more years, 18 years total, your money will double again. Thus $100,000 becomes $200,000 in nine years and $400,000 in 18 years because the $200,000 will double again in the second nine years. Money in tax deferred accounts double even faster because you do not need to worry about paying taxes on your annual returns.

7. Back to the Gift to Mom. In the above example, the gift to mom was outright (i.e., mom receives the money in one check and puts it into her own Trust (or his second spouse spends it on a really nice vacation, car—you name it). An outright gift to mom qualifies for the marital deduction. However, suppose this is a second marriage for dad and while he wants to take care of mom while she is alive, he wants to make sure that the principal—here, the $825,000—is left for his kids from his first marriage. Is there any way to limit mom's rights without jeopardizing the marital deduction? Note: again, we are assuming dad dies first, but the same applies if mom dies first.

First, it should be noted that there are various types of Marital Trusts that qualify for the marital deduction. These provide for (a) income to spouse and (b) allow the spouse to use or consume the principal; and (c) allow the spouse to choose who will receive the assets when the spouse dies. Other flexibility can be built into these Trusts. The powers can be very liberal because the amount in the Marital Trust will be included in the surviving spouse's estate and subject to taxation, just like the outright gift to the surviving spouse.

However, a Marital Trust with these liberal powers for the surviving spouse is not usually desirable in a second marriage situation. Instead, you want to control who gets the assets when your wife or husband dies after you, rather than that control being in their hands. A special type of Marital Trust exists that allows you that flexibility. It is called a Qualified Terminable Interest Property Trust (QTIP). Its characteristics are very similar to the Family Trust except that (1) much more than the exempt amount (currently $675,000) can be put into the QTIP Trust; and (2) the assets of the QTIP will be included in the surviving spouse's estate. In all cases, the surviving spouse must receive the income from the QTIP; any other rights are totally in your discretion.

Why is the QTIP Trust so popular? Because it qualifies your assets for the marital deduction but does not give the surviving spouse the right to choose who will get those assets when the surviving spouse dies. You make that decision up front. Therefore, the QTIP Trust solves the second-marriage problem: it allows you to transfer your property to the children of your first marriage when the second spouse dies. While the second spouse is alive, he or she will receive the income; thanks to the tax code, this special Trust qualifies for the marital deduction. Hence, there are no estate taxes upon the death of the first spouse, and you make sure your kids from the first marriage end up with the money when the second spouse passes away.

There is a second reason why you may want to have a Marital Trust (again, a QTIP Trust is one form of a Marital Trust): the generation skipping tax. A detailed discussion of the generation skipping tax is beyond the scope of this book. Suffice it to say that there is a separate tax—called the generation skipping tax—on distributions of assets to persons more than one generation below the person making the gift (e.g. a gift of $100,000 from grandmother to her grandson). However, each person has a $1,000,000 exemption, which is indexed for inflation. If you give a gift to your spouse outright, you waste that exemption on the amount on those assets. However, the IRS allows you to make a special election to use part of your exemption on assets left in a qualifying Marital Trust.

A second note: There is a second kind of special marital deduction Trust called the Qualified Domestic Trust ("QDOT"). A detailed discussion of these Trusts is beyond the scope of this book. Generally, the rules are as follows. If your spouse is not a U.S. citizen, transfers to her during your lifetime or at your death will not qualify for the estate tax marital deduction—unless you transfer assets to a QDOT. Therefore, unless a QDOT is used, federal taxes will be owed on gifts to your spouse—a negative result, to say the least. A QDOT requires that the Trustee be an U.S. citizen or U.S. corporate trustee, that all income is paid at least annually to the surviving spouse, and that numerous other conditions be satisfied. Moreover, a federal estate tax is imposed on the value of Trust assets when the surviving spouse dies or the QDOT fails to meet any requirement, or if the QDOT distributes anything other than Trust income to the surviving spouse.

8. When the Surviving Spouse Dies. As you can see, with careful planning, a substantial amount of estate taxes can be saved. Essentially, with good planning, $1,350,000 can pass tax free to your children or other loved ones; by 2006, that number will increase to $2,000,000—one million per person based on the increase in the exemption amount. And, as we discussed, this amount will increase if the amount in the Family Trust increases while mom is alive—remember the rule of 72s. Once the $675,000 in the Family Trust is exempted from federal estate taxes, that amount and the growth in the principal being held in trust while the surviving spouse is alive will escape taxation. Thus, hundreds of thousands of dollars in taxes can be saved.

For the sake of completeness, we want to briefly discuss what happens to the assets when the surviving spouse dies. The options here are virtually limitless. Let's assume this is a second marriage, with a Family Trust and a Marital QTIP Trust. Assuming there was $1,350,000 in dad's Living Trust, $675,000 went to the Family Trust and $675,000 went into the QTIP Trust. Assume the assets in the Family Trust grow at an average rate of five percent (5%) per year even though the new spouse was receiving income, and that the QTIP amount did not increase at all. Suppose the new spouse lived for fourteen (14) years and died. At that point, the $675,000 in the Family Trust would be worth $1,350,000, which would then pass to the children from the first marriage, as discussed below. The $675,000 in the QTIP would be subject to taxation but because it is worth less than the then applicable exempt amount of $1,000,000—remember it is past 2006— the entire amount escapes taxation. Usually that amount would be added to the Family Trust and then distributed under the first spouse's wishes. Hence, $2,025,000 is passing free of estate taxation to the kids.

How should the money be distributed to the kids? As discussed, the options are virtually limitless. In many cases, if the children are older, the kids' shares are distributed outright. Moreover, the plan usually provides that the share that any deceased's child receives is their parent's share—which raises a whole host of issues, not the least of which is how to decide when the kids are old enough to handle the money.

You can tailor the Living Trust to do virtually anything. One common scheme is to divide the money into equal shares for the kids and delay the distribution of money until the children are able to handle the responsibility—e.g., give each child the right to receive their assets as follows: one-third (1/3) at 25, one-third (1/3) at 30 and one-third (1/3) at 35, with the Successor Trustee having the authority to make distributions of principal earlier for worthy reasons such as education, starting a business or to cover medical expenses. Obviously, if your children are older, delayed distributions do not come into play; however, they will come into play if a child dies before receiving all of his or her share, which would go to the child's children (your grandchildren). Also, a contingent distribution to a charity or to remote relatives should be put into place in case all of your immediate family has passed away. Graphically, the Living Trust might look as follows:

Sample Living Trust

TRUST ASSETS
(After Payment of Debts and Expenses)

Family Trust

- Sheltered from taxes by unified credit ($675,000-$1,000,000)
- Surviving spouse may receive net income
- Trustee may distribute principal to surviving spouse or Settlor's descendants for health, support, maintenance, and education
- Trustee may distribute principal to Settlor's descendants for special projects
- Otherwise, principal is distributed to Settlor's descendants upon death of the surviving spouse

Outright to Surviving Spouse or into Marital Trust

- Both qualify for marital deduction
- Marital Trust:
  - Surviving Spouse receives all net income
  - Trustee may distribute principal to surviving spouse to maintain standard of living
  - Usually limited power of appointment to Settlor's descendants
  - Otherwise, principal is distributed to Settlor's descendants outright or via issue trusts

Trust for Descendants

- Income distributions discretionary prior to 21
- Income distributions at least annually after 21
- Distribution of principal as determined by Settlor (e.g. 1/3 at 30, 1/3 at 35, 1/3 at 40)
- Distribution of principal at Trustee's discretion for education, health, special projects and additional support
- Power of appointment to Settlor's descendants if die before receiving all assets

Contingency Clause

If no descendants or all descendants die, assets distributed to relatives or charities

As you can see, we have now built an entire Living Trust that (a) saves your family hundreds of thousands of tax dollars; (b) allows you to control who receives your money and when; and (c) covers numerous contingencies that might well occur during your life or the lives of your children. The Living Trust is truly a powerful tool that will take care of you and your family.

X.

<u>A LITTLE BIT MORE ABOUT PROBATE</u>

Now that we have discussed the benefits and details of the Living Trust, let's take a closer look at probate. First, a word of caution: the probate procedures, while similar in most states, do vary from state to state. Some states have recently adopted procedures to simplify the probate procedure for certain people in certain situations. A detailed discussion of any state's procedures is beyond the scope of this book. Again, while these new procedures have been designed to decrease expenses for the average person, it is our belief that it is still more cost-effective and more efficient for most people to establish a Living Trust. Or, as someone once said about the inventions in the dental profession, just because having cavities filled is less painful today due to new technology and procedures, doesn't mean that you want to get cavities.

What follows is a brief discussion of traditional probate because that is generally the same in all states. However, be aware that there may be other procedures available in your state that may be different from those discussed which may be appropriate for your situation.

Is Probate Necessary?   In most cases, no. However, hundreds of years ago, it was necessary. You see, back then, it took a long time to find people and notify them that someone they knew had died and left them an old watch. Today, traditional probate is almost as obsolete as the Pony Express, vinyl records or spats.

If your name is on the title of an asset when you die, probate is the legal way to change ownership of that asset. Probate officially takes your name off the title of an asset and puts someone else's name on it. So, don't you think it makes sense to avoid or minimize that step?

A will by itself is not enough authority to retitle assets or release the contents of bank accounts. A court order may be required depending on the circumstances. That court order is part of the traditional probate process. Effectively, however, after you die, your heirs may not be able to transfer title of your assets into their names without court involvement, and that usually means time and expense.

Simply writing a will isn't enough to proclaim its legality. Your will must be validated as being authentic before any assets can be transferred to your heirs. Probate is the only way to accomplish that main objective.

How Does Probate Start?   When you die, a representative of your estate must notify the court of your passing and usually must petition the court to initiate probate proceedings. The intent is to release assets and property that are titled in your name and transfer them in an orderly manner to your survivors.

Your signature controls many material goods and personal belongings that are important in your day-to-day life. Once you're gone, those possessions may not be available to your spouse and family. That could include your bank accounts, vehicles, land, homes and investments.

Unfortunately, the process of probate may be incredibly inefficient in performing its job of transferring ownership, and it may be time consuming and expensive.

What Really Happens in Probate?   The actual way probate works is slightly different from state to state, and even from court to court.   But, generally, traditional probate performs the same functions.

1.   A representative of your estate asks the court to start probate proceedings.   This person will normally be the person you've chosen as your executor or Personal Representative.   If you don't have a will, or if your will is invalidated, the court will appoint an executor or Personal Representative for you.

2.   The court takes control of your estate in traditional probate; in informal probate, the personal representative will have a lot more control.   If your widow needs to have access to something, she may have to petition the court to place it into traditional probate.   As previously mentioned, for that reason, some states have what's called an "independent probate," or "informal probate" which minimizes court interference for less complicated estates.

3.   At the first hearing, the judge will generally settle four matters, assuming the will is not contested:

> If your will is valid

> If it is the correct will

> If you were competent when you signed it

> If it is properly signed and witnessed or authenticated

If the judge decides that any of those four elements is not satisfied, he may officially declare that you actually died without a valid will, or intestate—and distribute your assets under the laws of the state in which you live—usually not a desirable outcome since your distribution scheme will likely not be the same as the "will the state made for you" under state law.   Fortunately, this does not happen too often if you have worked with a competent estate planning professional.

In informal procedures, it is essentially assumed that these criteria are satisfied and the burden is upon persons interested in your estate to challenge your will and prove it is flawed by bringing it to the Court's attention in the first place.

4.   The judge officially appoints an executor or Personal Representative for your estate.

5.   The court starts supervising the payment of your debts—either directly or indirectly—if any claims are filed against your estate.

6.   Most states in America require an official notice to appear in a newspaper. It announces your death and, some people argue, almost invites your creditors to present their claims on your property.   Creditors usually have four to six months to file claims.

7.   Your executor or Personal Representative will prepare an inventory of all assets you own, which in a traditional probate will be filed with the Court; the executor or Personal Representative may need to hire an appraiser to value some of your assets.

8.   Your executor or Personal Representative pays your final bills, which may be submitted to the court for approval.

9.   Your executor or Personal Representative applies for and collects death benefits from life insurance coverage to which your estate is entitled.

10.   Your executor or Personal Representative arranges to have your final tax returns prepared. These include your final income tax return and any state and federal estate tax returns that need to be filed.

11.   A final hearing is held to settle your estate. At this hearing, the judge reviews the paperwork and orders (or approves) your debts paid if they have not already been paid. These debts include attorney fees, executor fees, appraisal fees (if any) and all probate expenses. As we discussed previously, these expenses can be substantial. If there isn't enough cash in your estate to pay these

expenses, the judge can order some or all of your assets sold to pay them. All remaining assets will then be distributed according to the terms in your will.

12. Finally, your executor is released from his or her duties and your file is closed.

13. Note: If you own property in another state, your family will probably have to go through probate in the other state before your property in that state can be turned over to your family. They will have to deal with other jurisdictions, other processes, other people and other fee schedules. That's probate.

Many people complain about Probate Court. Those complaints are really not well founded because you have the ability to avoid probate by taking care of your matters while you are alive. Believe us, there is not a Probate Judge alive who takes great pleasure in handling the routine matters that come before the court—such as annual accountings—that could have been avoided. That is not to say that they don't want to handle them; only that it is not the most important and stimulating part of their job. Call it a necessary evil.

However, if you fail to take care of your affairs by setting up a Living Trust and first-class estate plan, the probate court provides a very useful function—it allows your affairs to be wrapped up and your assets transferred to your loved ones. It appoints a conservator and guardian if you neglect to have a Durable Power of Attorney and/or a Living Trust. Thus, it acts as a great safety net if you fail to handle your affairs; however, just like that other great safety net—unemployment compensation—just because we have it does not mean that we want to use it.

In short, while probate is now more tolerable in some states than it was before, the entire probate process, and its attendant expense, can be easily avoided with a well-prepared estate plan that includes as its central document, a Living Trust. In those states without the new procedures, it is simply as intolerable as it has always been in the past.

XI.

TRANSFERRING ASSETS AND FUNDING THE LIVING TRUST

Let's take a quick look at assets that do not go through probate. As you know, not everything you own will automatically go through probate.

How Property Passes to Your Beneficiary

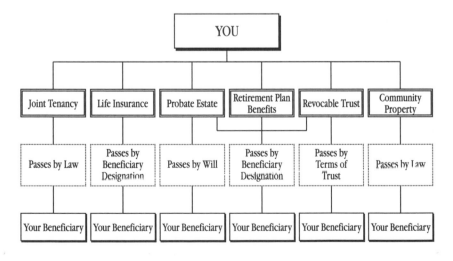

1.   Assets that you own together (jointly) with your spouse will probably transfer directly to her without going through probate. Of course, that requires that they be legally owned by both of you with rights of survivorship. As previously discussed, a better approach is usually to put those assets into a Living Trust for one of you, particularly if your assets are in excess of $675,000 (the exempt amount). However, jointly owned properties have a number of other problems, as discussed elsewhere, including the specter of going through probate in the event both of you pass away together—for example, in a car accident. As previously discussed, jointly held assets with your children raises another whole host of problems.

2.   Assets (such as insurance policies) that have a valid and correctly named primary beneficiary and contingent beneficiary will go directly to your beneficiary, bypassing probate, if the beneficiary is alive. So, if your wife is the beneficiary of your insurance policy, she will receive the money without it passing through probate. In the typical estate plan, where saving taxes is not a major issue, the Living Trust should be the contingent beneficiary because the terms of the Living Trust will then control who gets your assets and when. In addition, as discussed, it is desirable to avoid having your estate be a contingent beneficiary because then your insurance proceeds can be used to pay claims of creditors, which would not be the case if the Living Trust were named as contingent beneficiary.

As previously discussed, the rules regarding naming the Living Trust as the primary or contingent beneficiary of your retirement plans (401(k), IRAs and 403(b) accounts) should be reviewed with your estate planning professional to make sure the beneficiary designations work properly with your overall estate plan; however, all things being equal—and they rarely are—the spouse is usually the primary beneficiary.

Remember that a Living Trust can not work properly without the assets being put into the Trust. Therefore, the transfer of assets and beneficiary designations should be executed at the same time as the Living Trust is signed or shortly thereafter. We can not tell you how many times we have run across a Living Trust that has been executed but has not been funded at all—a total waste of money.

XII.

PAY ME NOW OR PAY ME LATER: FIND A GOOD ESTATE PLANNING LAWYER NOW

Quite amazingly to us, 70% of all people will die without having any estate plan in place. This number is staggering, considering that the cost of preparing a relatively sophisticated estate plan has decreased dramatically because of advancements in technology and increased specialization in the practice of law.

The estate planning lawyer is like the Fram oil filter guy: either pay him now or pay him later. When you pay him later, it's going to be a lot more expensive because it's going to take a lot more work to sort out the many problems that you could have eliminated at very little expense. Moreover, even with the simplified probate procedures, there will be more time and expense incurred than there would be if you had taken the time to take care of these problems on the front end.

We believe that one of the major reasons people do not institute estate plans is because they don't know how to find the right estate planning lawyer. Accordingly, we have devoted this chapter to providing some practical advice as to how you should retain a capable estate planning lawyer who will work with you.

How do you locate a qualified and knowledgeable estate planning lawyer? Looking in the yellow pages is probably not the answer because the listings aren't going to give you much information. The lawyers prepare the ads themselves so there is no guaranty that a lawyer will be an expert in every area listed in the ad.

Another option is to try some of the lawyer referral sources, but, again, lawyers subscribe to these services. While these resources may be better indicators than mere advertisements, they still are services that may be supported by attorneys themselves. However, most referral resources perform at least some due diligence on the attorneys; the AARP is a referral source that carries out due diligence on its lawyers.

An excellent approach for finding a practiced estate planning lawyer is to ask another lawyer you trust for a referral to an experienced estate planning lawyer. Lawyers usually know which lawyers are first-rate and honest. Ask your lawyer if his own estate plan was prepared by the referred lawyer. That is a good litmus test. Unfortunately, many of you may not know a lawyer to ask for a referral.

The most practical solution, for most of you, is probably to talk to somebody in the financial services industry. Our recommendation is that the person be your life insurance agent, financial planner, stockbroker, or even your accountant (if you have one). These people work with estate planning lawyers much more frequently than you do. They know whether the attorney is not only competent, but trustworthy and likeable as well, and they should know whether this lawyer will respond to the client on a timely basis and work diligently to conclude the estate plan within a reasonable time after the attorney is engaged. Most important, these people are accessible to you; namely, you probably see one or more of these people on a regular basis.

Once you secure the attorney's name, you should meet with him or her to see if that individual is right for you. Most attorneys do not charge for the initial consultation, but to be certain, inquire when you set up the appointment. Then, meet with the lawyer to see if you can work together. During the initial meeting—call it an interview—you should observe whether the lawyer satisfies the **"Three Cs: competence, compatibility and cost."** Let's discuss these in detail.

First, the lawyer must be a competent estate planning practitioner. There are lawyers in firms, both large and small, that devote a substantial amount of their practice to estate planning. You should only hire the person when you are confident that he or she has the expertise to handle your estate plan. Regardless of how you come to find a lawyer, we suggest that you ask that person, point blank, how many estate plans they've prepared or drafted.

Second, you must be compatible with the lawyer. During your first meeting, you should evaluate whether you are like-minded. Do you trust him? Do you want this lawyer to be the person your spouse calls when you pass away? Do you get along and perhaps even like him—heaven forbid? Within a very short period of time, you are going to be telling this person some very important things about yourself, including how much you are worth and to whom you want to leave your assets. If the answer to any of these questions is "no," do not hire that lawyer. Remember that you are not getting a document, you are beginning a relationship. The lawyer will be talking for you after you are gone. If you're not comfortable with this lawyer, for whatever reason, find someone else.

The third criterion is cost. Most lawyers at the big firms work on an hourly basis. Lawyers in smaller firms usually work on a fixed fee basis. Make sure you find out on what basis the lawyer charges fees. However, you need to be fair. Any competent lawyer will want to know the complexity of your estate plan before a quote is given. Do you need a Cadillac or a Yugo? The price is not the same. For example, someone who need a separate, stylized subtrust for each child is going to pay more than the person who needs a Family Trust that will cover all the kids.

We want to point out a couple observations about costs. First, contrary to popular belief, the cost of a "simple will" is not always materially different than the cost of a complete estate planning package that includes a Living Trust. The reason is that the attorney's start up time is the same in either event and, with computers, the time spent drafting the document may not be materially different for a will and a Living Trust. Second, the cost may be higher if the attorney helps with the beneficiary designations, but in our judgment, the assistance is worth the extra cost. Remember without funding, the Living Trust is not worth the paper on which it is written. Note: some lawyers may not help with beneficiary designations.

Third, one of the major reasons that Living Trusts are usually cheaper than going through probate is that you are doing the work to re-register your assets, whereas a Personal Representative will charge you. Moreover, since you are obviously familiar with your affairs, you can retitle your assets and change your beneficiary designations more efficiently.

In sum, your estate planning attorney should be someone you like, someone competent, and someone you can afford. You deserve no less.

XIII.

QUESTIONS & ANSWERS

Q1. What exactly is a Living Trust?

A.   It is a "paper person" that is legally separate from you. This separate "person" is set up to hold and manage assets, property and funds for you. Since it's separate from you, when you transfer ownership of your property to its name, you are no longer the owner. When you are no longer the owner, probate is bypassed.

The Living Trust dictates who receives your property when you die. It also dictates how and when those people will receive the property. It lets you distribute your property in whatever proportions you wish. It even allows you to disinherit anyone you wish to "cut out."

Q2. What's the difference between a will and a Living Trust?

A.   Both are written legal documents intended to let you specify how your property will pass to your heirs when you die. However, when you rely on a will only, your property must pass through probate in order for it to be transferred to your heirs. When you rely on a Living Trust, your property bypasses probate and goes directly to your heirs.

Q3. What happens to my property if I die without a will?

A. Dying without a valid will is called dying "intestate." Under those circumstances, the court follows a statute set by the legislature in your state to determine who inherits what assets. This statute usually distributes the property based on family relationships. By drawing up a valid will, you usually dictate who receives what assets. Without a valid will, your wishes are ignored, and your assets are distributed as if you died without a will.

Q4. I have heard about people having problems with a Living Trust. How can I avoid that?

A. If anyone has a problem with a Living Trust, it's probably because his or her property was left out of the Trust. That exposes them to probate. The simple solution is to simply place your assets into your Living Trust.

Q5. What are the reasons for NOT having a Living Trust?

A. Homelessness and poverty—just kidding. Even if you think your estate is small, you should talk to an experienced estate planning attorney to see if your assets are so few and your affairs are so simple that a Living Trust is not appropriate for you. For most attorneys that initial consultation is free.

Q6. Does transferring property into a Living Trust cause a reappraisal of the property so that property taxes are increased?

A. No. A transfer into a Revocable Living Trust generally does not produce a reappraisal or revaluation of the property for tax purposes.

Q7. Can I sell assets or add new assets to my Living Trust?

A. Yes, you can. You can sell assets and add new assets all by yourself without requiring a change of the Trust. In effect, you can do anything you want with your property while it is in the Trust and still retain control over your assets.

Q8. Should I add my son's name to the deeds to my property?

A.   No. This is a very serious point. Never add another person's name to any property; usually you should put that property into your Living Trust instead. As we discussed, putting your son's name on your assets causes you and your family some serious problems, including gift tax problems, loss of control to your son and creating risk of claims from his creditors.

Q9. I'm not sure about whom to name as my Trustee. My only child is irresponsible and in the midst of a nasty divorce.

A.   Your Trustee should be a responsible adult who is capable of acting on your behalf to fulfill your wishes at your death or incapacity. Make sure that person's own name is not on the title to any of the property in your Trust. Without title to the assets in your Trust, your Trustee could go through a divorce, bankruptcy or litigation, and it would not affect your assets. In addition, you could hire an institutional Trustee, such as a bank, if your assets are sufficient. Institution Trustees do a great job, particularly when the beneficiaries do not have a close relationship or have competing interests. Remember they have the most experience in those situations since they have been handling Trust accounts for years.

Q10.   Can a Living Trust reduce my income taxes while I am alive?

A.   No. A Living Trust gives you no special **income** tax advantages. You will be required to pay all the income taxes you legally owe. However, as we discussed, a Living Trust can save you a substantial amount of federal and state estate taxes.

Q11.   What's the process for putting my assets into my Living Trust? Is it difficult?

A.   Don't worry; it's a simple process, and there are no fees involved, except for minor recording fees for transferring property into the Trust via a deed. You place assets into your Trust by changing the name on all your valuables and all your titled and fixed assets.

- Valuables include: art, household items and jewelry.

- Titled assets include: annuities, life insurance, savings accounts, money markets, stocks, mutual funds, CDs, bonds.

- Fixed assets include land.

The titled and fixed assets are transferred into the name of your Living Trust. This is the most important step in the process. Only by transferring them to your Trust can they truly avoid the probate process.

AARP says, "Remember that simply writing a trust document will not help you avoid probate. Until you transfer ownership of your property to the trust, the trust is not worth any more to you (or your beneficiaries) than the paper it is printed on."

Q12.   What happens if there's a problem with my will?

A.   If the court deems that your will is not valid for any reason, it will probably "ride herd" over your estate as if you had never written a will. That is the worst of all worlds. Therefore, you should make sure you hire an experienced estate planning lawyer.

Q13.   Should I write a will when I establish my Living Trust?

A.   Yes. A will, called a "Pour Over Will," is one of the most important things in your estate plan. If, for some reason, you did not transfer all your assets into the Trust, the Pour Over Will picks up those overlooked assets when you die and transfers them into your Trust. However, all assets transferred to your Trust by that Pour Over Will must go through the probate process. It is best to put all your assets into the Trust initially.

Q14.   When I set up my Living Trust, will I need to apply for a special tax status?

A.   No. You will not need a special taxpayer identification number or a special tax form.

Q15.   Will my tax status change when I create a Living Trust?

A.   Not as long as you are the owner/Grantor and income beneficiary of your Trust. Any incomes generated by assets owned in your Living Trust are taxed as if they were still held in your name. They are reported on your personal 1040 form.

Q16.   My investments did not perform well for me. Can I borrow against the assets in my Living Trust?

A.   Yes, you can. A Living Trust does not restrict your rights to borrow against the assets in any way. The bank may ask to see a copy of the Trust, however.

Q17.   What rights does my wife have regarding the assets in my Trust?

A.   Each of you has independent access to any Trust account in both your names. It's the same as having a joint account. However, if you and she have separate Living Trusts (which is usually preferable) neither of you will have rights to the other's Living Trust, unless you are co-Trustees of each other's Trusts.

Q18.   Who manages a Living Trust?

A.   You would normally control and manage your own Trust. Your wife would control and manage hers. However, each of you can legally name anyone you trust to manage your separate Trust(s). It can be a relative, a friend or a bank.

Q19.   Are Living Trusts recognized in all 50 states?

A.   Yes. Living Trusts are recognized as legal and valid in every state.

Q20.   Will I be required to rewrite my Trust if I divorce?

A.   The Trust, as all documents and assets, should more than likely be thoroughly reviewed by the divorce attorneys. They would probably recommend the appropriate modifications for you and your soon-to-be ex-wife.

Q21.   When should I update my Living Trust?

A.   Since your Living Trust is a legal document, make sure to review it with the professional who set it up for you. It is a good idea to review it at least once every three to five years to make certain it still represents exactly what you want. Two types of circumstances could suggest an update.

1)   You might want to change your Trust if any major events have occurred in your life: marriage, divorce, death, birth, legal problems, bankruptcy or winning the lottery.

2)   You should consider making a change if the people you appointed as Successor Trustees can no longer fulfill their responsibilities.

Q22.   I own a Living Trust. How and when will it end?

A.   Your Living Trust will end in one of two ways:

1) It may be revoked by you as the owner/Grantor at any time.

2) It will be terminated when all of the assets have been distributed.

Q23.   Does a Living Trust give my estate protection from my creditors?

A.   A Living Trust does not buffer your assets from the claims of legitimate creditors, except for certain assets, such as life insurance, which are payable directly to your Successor Trustee.

Q24.   My only heir is my 16-year-old daughter. Can I appoint her as my Successor Trustee?

A.   No. A Successor Trustee must be at least 18 years old.

Q25.   What is the difference between "Revocable" and "Irrevocable" Trusts?

A. These Trusts are the exact opposite of each other. Revocable Trusts can be changed or modified at any time by the owner (you) until incapacity or death occurs. Irrevocable Trusts cannot be changed once they have been created.

Q26. If I want to buy a new piece of property, how do I arrange it with my Living Trust?

A. The property should probably be purchased in the name of the Trust. At the time of purchase, give the seller the information about your Trust so the original paperwork will be in the name of your Trust.

Q27. What is an A-B Trust?

A. An A-B Trust is the name given to a version of a Living Trust that is used by married couples to minimize estate taxes. See Chapter IX.

Q28. Where does probate take place?

A. Probate takes place in the city or county where you have your permanent, legal home, technically called your place of residence.

Q29. Is there anything bad about a Living Trust?

A. In our judgment, there is nothing bad about a Living Trust. It is a traditional estate planning tool that is steeped in legal precedence. For many middle-class people, it is the perfect way to protect family and assets.

©DG 1990

XIV.

<u>CONCLUSION</u>

Did you hear the joke: "What is the definition of insanity?"

Answer: "Doing the same thing over and over again and expecting the result to change!"

Don't be insane; doing nothing does not help you or your family.

Throughout these pages, you have discovered that you have some options for protecting your family, assets and property. The path you choose has a direct bearing on how you will be remembered. What do you want your family and friends to say about you after you're gone?

You can follow the traditional path, placing your family's fate in the hands of probate court. But the prevailing wisdom says that's not a particularly good choice. Or, you can take a different path and truly take care of your family and property. The most logical way to do that is with a Living Trust.

You have learned that there are many incredible benefits to having a Living Trust. Many experts think the most important benefit is the avoidance of your estate going through probate. However, you might think the biggest benefit is that a Living Trust can protect your family's lifestyle and dignity after you're gone. Or that it covers you in the event of disability.

We'd agree with you. However, regardless of the reason or reasons, you owe it to your family—the people you love.

The good news is that a Living Trust does all of the above.

However, in order to have that protection, you simply must take the first step. Just knowing about a Living Trust does you no good. You must make the decision to prepare one. You must pick up the phone and call an experienced estate planning lawyer. Putting it off only hurts your family because it forces them to handle matters later that you could have easily—and inexpensively—handled yourself in the present. Where's the pride in that?

As we stated at the beginning of the book, Gram Bert, who died recently at age 96, has a great expression to describe someone who does not do what they should: "he burned his butt and now he has to sit on the blisters." In other words, you made the mistake and now you have to live with the consequences. That great expression—which is the only time we have ever heard Gram Bert swear—contains more wisdom than the wisdom possessed by all the law professors at Michigan Law School. And it fits perfectly here too. There is only one difference. If you do not take care of business now, **your family** will bear the consequences later. You don't want that to be your legacy. Act now and feel that sense of accomplishment and relief.

XV.

EPILOGUE:
THE TAX ACT OF 2001

President Bush recently signed into law the Economic Growth and Tax Relief and Reconciliation Act of 2001. The most significant changes are set forth below.

Beginning on January 1, 2002, the exemption from federal estate and gift tax is increased and the top estate and gift tax is reduced. Below is a chart showing the estate tax exemption and top estate and gift tax rates for calendar years 2002-2011.

Calendar Year	Estate Tax Exemption	Highest Estate and Gift Tax Rates
2002	$1 million	50%
2003	$1 million	49%
2004	$1.5 million	48%
2005	$1.5 million	47%
2006	$2 million	46%
2007	$2 million	45%
2008	$2 million	45%
2009	$3.5 million	45%
2010	Estate tax and generation skipping tax are repealed for one year	0%
2011	$1 million	55%

In 2010, for one year only, the estate tax has been repealed. The estate tax is reinstated on January 1, 2011, absent further Congressional action.

The gift tax is not repealed. Starting in 2002, it is continued with a $1 million exemption and a top rate of tax which is equal to the top federal income tax rate (scheduled to be 35%). Note that the gift tax exemption will not increase over time. Thus, beginning on January 1, 2004, the estate tax exemption will be larger than the gift tax exemption. In addition, starting in 2004, the generation skipping tax exemption will be equal to the estate tax exemption.

In 2010, the year that the estate tax is repealed, it is replaced with a capital gains tax. Under current law, all assets which have appreciated during an individual's lifetime receive a "step-up" in basis to the value of the assets on the individual's date of death. In 2010 only, the tax law removes the "step-up" basis. Therefore, any built-in capital gains will not be eliminated for the year 2010. This is known as "carryover basis" (i.e. the basis will remain the amount an individual paid when he purchased the property). Under the new law, there will be an exemption for the first $1,300,000 in lifetime gain for a single person and an additional exemption for the first $3,000,000 in lifetime gain for assets transferred to a surviving spouse.

As a result of these changes in the tax laws, several things are apparent. First, all of the primary reasons for having a Living Trust are still valid. Second, fewer people will now need to use Living Trusts to save federal and estate taxes because the exemption amount is higher ($1,000,000 starting in 2002).

The estate planning techniques in Chapter IX are still valid, except that instead of the first $675,000 being exempt, $1 Million will be exempt in 2002, which amount eventually increases to $3.5 Million by year 2009. Remember with proper planning, a married couple can take advantage of both exemptions for a husband and wife, as we discussed in Chapter IX. For example, in 2002, a married couple will be able to transfer $2 Million tax free to their heirs; in 2007 that amount is $7 Million.

Third, existing estate planning documents should be reviewed and updated. For example, those documents may have had certain provisions that were needed to save taxes under the old law, which are no longer necessary because of the increased exemption. Moreover, if your current estate plan leaves the exemption amount to someone other than a trust for your spouse, (e.g. a family trust), these tax law changes may cause an inadvertent result of significantly fewer assets being available to benefit your spouse.

In sum, under the new tax laws, a Living Trust is still superior to a simple will for estate planning purposes. Many commentators, including ourselves, believe that the federal estate tax will never be completely eliminated. Nevertheless, the new changes are a step in the right direction because the increases in the exempt amount will eliminate estate taxes for most Americans. Even without estate taxes to worry about, the Living Trust is still the tool of choice to pass on wealth to the next generation.

GLOSSARY

Set forth below are definitions of some key terms, expressed in plain English.

Administration: Court supervised handling of an estate during the probate process.

Administrator: A person appointed by the court to manage your estate under two conditions: 1) if you die without a valid will; and 2) if you don't name an executor.

Ancillary Administration: A probate proceeding in a state other than your home state, also known as your state of residence. When you own real estate or other titled assets in more than one state at the time of your death, your family may face multiple probate proceedings. They usually run concurrently.

Beneficiary: A person who is receiving or designated to receive a benefit, advantage or profits under a legal instrument such as a Trust, estate, insurance policy or retirement plan.

Codicil: A written addition, supplement or amendment to an existing will. It is a separate legal document that must be properly witnessed and executed.

Community Property: Property that is owned in common by husband and wife with each having an undivided one-half interest in the property because of their marital status. In common law jurisdictions, one-half of what is earned by one spouse is the property of the other spouse. Most common in western states such as California, Arizona, Washington and Nevada, among others.

Competent: Technically means capable of doing something. In estate planning, a person is competent to make a will if the person understands the nature and extent of his property and can identify the objects of his bounty (to whom he wants to give his property) and can understand the consequences of his making a will.

Conservatorship: A formal proceeding in which the court appoints a person (called as conservator) to act as the agent of another person with respect to such person's property; such person acts as a fiduciary for the benefit of that person, taking care of that person's property.

Contingent Beneficiary: A person who receives a benefit or assets only if the primary beneficiary is deceased at the time the assets are distributed.

Corpus: Property owned by your Trust, commonly referred to as "corpus of the Trust." Also known as the principal of the Trust. In contrast, the earnings of the Trust is commonly called income or earnings of the Trust.

Death Taxes: Amounts levied on the property of the deceased. Called estate taxes (federal) and inheritance (state) taxes.

Creator: The person who creates a Trust. Also known as the Grantor or Settlor.

Decedent: This is a legal term for someone who has died. A deceased person.

Devise: A gift of real estate made by will.

Durable (financial) Power of Attorney: A power of attorney is a legal document that authorizes someone to make financial decisions on your behalf. It is called "durable" because it will continue to be valid if you become incapacitated or incompetent. It is created while you are competent.

Estate: An estate is usually considered the assets, real estate and personal property that you own at the time of death.

Estate Tax: An estate tax is a tax upon the transfer of property by the decedent upon his or her death. Estate taxes are based on the right to transfer property while inheritance taxes are based on the right to receive the property.

Execute: The act(s) necessary to make a document valid. Usually is the act of signing (and in some cases witnessing and notarizing) the particular document.

Executor/Executrix or Personal Representative: A person or an institution named in a will or appointed by the probate court to carry out the instructions of the will. The person is in charge of probating the decedent's estate.

Funding: The process of transferring ownership of property from your personal name into the name of your Living Trust (a/k/a "John Smith, as initial Trustee of the John Smith Living Trust U/A/D _____"). Funding effectively allows property in a Living Trust to avoid probate.

Grantor: You, the person who creates a Trust. Also known as Creator or Settlor.

Guardian: Person who is legally responsible for the care and management of a person who cannot act for himself or herself. The person who manages the assets of the person is known as the conservator in some states.

Heir: A person who is legally entitled to inherit property from an individual who has died without a valid will or intestate.

Inter vivos: "Between the living" or "while living."

Intestate: The legal status of someone who dies without a valid will.

Irrevocable Trust: A Trust that cannot be changed, amended or modified once it is established, except by reformation by the court.

Joint Tenancy: A form of property ownership. When two or more people own property together in such a way that any one of them can act as owner of the whole (i.e. have the use and enjoyment of the entire property while alive).

Joint Tenancy with a Right of Survivorship: A type of ownership in which two or more people own the same property, and when one joint tenant dies, full ownership passes automatically and completely to the surviving joint tenant(s).

Life Interest: An interest in property, which terminates upon the death of the holder.

Living Trust: A Trust established while you are alive and which becomes effective while you are alive. It remains under your control until death. It then allows property in the Trust to pass to beneficiaries of the Trust free of probate.

Living Will: A document used to state your wishes about whether to use, withhold, or withdraw medical treatment, such as life support systems, when you become terminally ill.

Marital Deduction: Exempts from federal estate tax all property passing from one spouse to the other by reason of gift or death.

Medical Durable Power of Attorney: A power of attorney that is created while you are competent. It authorizes someone you trust to make health-care decisions when you are unable to do so on your own. Also known as a Healthcare Power of Attorney or Patient Advocate Form.

Non-probate Property: Property, such as life insurance benefits, retirement benefits, property held in joint tenancy with a right of survivorship, and property held in trust that is usually not subject to the probate process.

Per Capita: A Latin term that generally means "through the head;" anything divided based on a per capita basis is computed by dividing such amount equally by the number of heads (or individuals).

Per Stirpes: A Latin term generally meaning that your heirs will receive "by right of representation" their share of the inheritance that their immediate ancestor would have received if still living. In contrast, to distribution by per capita, which is equal division of the property to be divided by the number of beneficiaries, without referring to the immediate ancestors of such persons.

Personal Property: Generally speaking all tangible property—things that are movable. Includes items like jewelry, china, artwork, furniture, automobiles, guns and clothes. Excludes land and buildings attached to the land.

Personal Representative: The person named in a will or appointed by the court to represent an estate in the probate process.

Pour Over Will: This is a legal document that acts as a "catch-all" for anything you might have forgotten to place in your Living Trust. At your death the Pour Over Will effectively transfers to your Trust any property not previously placed there. However, all of that property must go through probate first.

Powers of Appointment: Power given to someone else to dispose of property or an interest in property.

Power of Attorney: A legal document whereby you authorize someone else to act for you as your agent.

Probate: A complex legal process which includes: determining the validity of a will, appointing an executor or personal representative, paying debts and taxes, identifying heirs and creditors and distributing property according to the dictates of a valid will.

Real Property: Land and whatever is constructed on or growing on land, as well as certain rights relating to land. Realty is an interest in land.

Revocable Living Trust: A Trust that takes effect in your lifetime. You can revoke, amend or terminate the terms of the Trust.

Revoke: To withdraw, rescind, terminate or cancel.

Settlor: You, the person who creates a Trust. Also called Grantor or Creator.

Successor Trustee: Individual or institution named in the Trust agreement who takes over management of Trust assets after the initial Trustee.

Tenancy in Common: A type of joint ownership in which two or more persons own a single property. While both joint tenants are alive, each has the right to possess and use the entire parcel. Each owner can dispose of his or her share at death without obtaining consent from other tenant(s).

Tenancy by the Entirety: Ownership of any type of property by a husband and wife together. The husband and wife are said to hold the property as one person. Upon the death of one spouse, the other owns the property alone like joint tenancy with rights of survivorship.

Testacy: Dying with a valid will in place. All property controlled by the will passes through probate, and the court determines the distribution of that property under the will.

Testator/Testatrix: The man or woman who executes a will.

Testamentary Trust: A Trust that takes effect at death, which is usually created by a valid will. Since all property controlled by the will passes through probate, all property controlled by the Testamentary Trust passes through probate, too.

Trust: A relationship under which one person holds property for the benefit of another person. Often created by a Trust Agreement that specifies the terms of the distribution of the benefits of the trust relationship. A trust relationship creates two interests: the Trustee, who holds the legal title to or interest in the property, and the beneficiary who has the equitable title or interest in or right to receive the property or other benefits held by the Trustee in trust.

Trustee: One who holds the legal title to property in trust for the benefit of another person. The Trustee is required by law to follow the terms of any Trust Agreement and to carry out the duties given to the person by the Settlor, the person who set up the Trust.

Uniform Probate Code: A model law that addresses the topics of probate law, asset transfer, guardianship and other matters. It is designed to serve as a model for states to make the laws of the various states more uniform.

Will: An instrument in which a person declares how he wants his property to be distributed after his death. This declaration can be changed, revoked or otherwise altered while alive. Also called Last Will and Testament.

NOTES